U0822113

中华人民共和国

2020年国民经济和社会发展统计公报

STATISTICAL COMMUNIQUÉ OF THE PEOPLE'S REPUBLIC OF CHINA ON THE 2020 NATIONAL ECONOMIC AND SOCIAL DEVELOPMENT

国 家 统 计 局
National Bureau of Statistics of China

2021年2月28日
February 28, 2021

中国统计出版社
China Statistics Press

图书在版编目（CIP）数据

中华人民共和国2020年国民经济和社会发展统计公报 = Statistical Communiqué of the People's Republic of China on the 2020 National Economic and Social Development : 汉英对照 / 国家统计局编 . -- 北京 : 中国统计出版社 , 2021.3
ISBN 978-7-5037-9461-2

Ⅰ . ①中… Ⅱ . ①国… Ⅲ . ①国民经济发展－统计资料－公报－中国－2020－汉、英②社会发展－统计资料－公报－中国－2020－汉、英 Ⅳ . ① F124-66

中国版本图书馆 CIP 数据核字 (2021) 第 034265 号

中华人民共和国2020年国民经济和社会发展统计公报

作　　者 / 国家统计局
责任编辑 / 郭 栋
装帧设计 / 黄 晨
出版发行 / 中国统计出版社
地　　址 / 北京市丰台区西三环南路甲6号　　邮政编码 /100073
网　　址 /http://www.zgtjcbs.com
电　　话 /（010）63376866　63376907（发行部）
印　　刷 / 北京画中画印刷有限公司
经　　销 / 新华书店
开　　本 /880×1230 毫米　1/16
字　　数 /92 千字
印　　张 /4.75
版　　别 /2021年3月第1版
版　　次 /2021年3月北京第1次印刷
定　　价 /38.00 元

版权所有。未经许可，本书的任何部分不准以任何方式在世界任何地区以任何文字翻印、拷贝、仿制或转载。
如有印装错误，本社发行部负责调换。

目录

CONTENTS

中华人民共和国
2020 年国民经济和社会发展统计公报[1]

国家统计局
2021 年 2 月 28 日

2020 年是新中国历史上极不平凡的一年。面对严峻复杂的国际形势、艰巨繁重的国内改革发展稳定任务特别是新冠肺炎疫情的严重冲击，以习近平同志为核心的党中央统揽全局，保持战略定力，准确判断形势，精心谋划部署，果断采取行动，付出艰苦努力，及时作出统筹疫情防控和经济社会发展的重大决策。各地区各部门坚持以习近平新时代中国特色社会主义思想为指导，全面贯彻党的十九大和十九届二中、三中、四中、五中全会精神，按照党中央、国务院决策部署，沉着冷静应对风险挑战，坚持高质量发展方向不动摇，统筹疫情防控和经济社会发展，扎实做好“六稳”工作，全面落实“六保”任务，我国经济运行逐季改善、逐步恢复常态，在全球主要经济体中唯一实现经济正增长，脱贫攻坚战取得全面胜利，决胜全面建成小康社会取得决定性成就，交出一份人民满意、世界瞩目、可以载入史册的答卷。

[1] 本公报中数据均为初步统计数。各项统计数据均未包括香港特别行政区、澳门特别行政区和台湾省。部分数据因四舍五入的原因，存在总计与分项合计不等的情况。

一、综合[2]

初步核算，全年国内生产总值[3]1015986亿元，比上年增长2.3%。其中，第一产业增加值77754亿元，增长3.0%；第二产业增加值384255亿元，增长2.6%；第三产业增加值553977亿元，增长2.1%。第一产业增加值占国内生产总值比重为7.7%，第二产业增加值比重为37.8%，第三产业增加值比重为54.5%。全年最终消费支出拉动国内生产总值下降0.5个百分点，资本形成总额拉动国内生产总值增长2.2个百分点，货物和服务净出口拉动国内生产总值增长0.7个百分点。分季度看，一季度国内生产总值同比下降6.8%，二季度增长3.2%，三季度增长4.9%，四季度增长6.5%。预计全年人均国内生产总值72447元，比上年增长2.0%。国民总收入[4]1009151亿元，比上年增长1.9%。全国万元国内生产总值能耗[5]比上年下降0.1%。预计全员劳动生产率[6]为117746元/人，比上年提高2.5%。

图1 2016–2020年国内生产总值及其增长速度

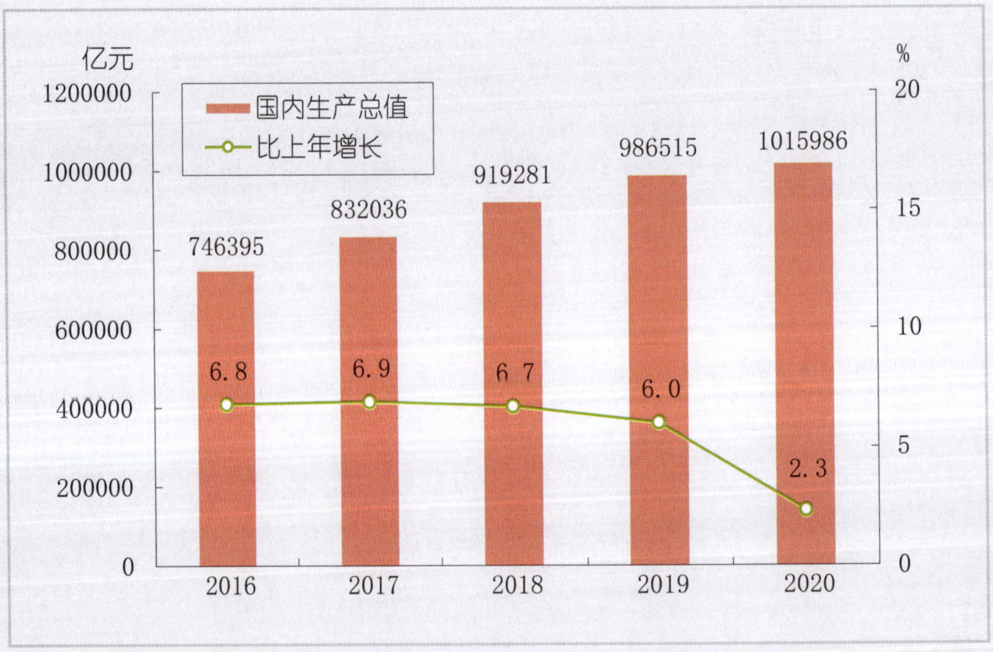

[2] 2020年开展第七次全国人口普查，相关数据拟于2021年4月份发布，公报中不再单独发布人口和就业人员相关数据。公报中涉及的人均指标根据人口预计数计算得到。

[3] 国内生产总值、三次产业及相关行业增加值、地区生产总值、人均国内生产总值和国民总收入绝对数按现价计算，增长速度按不变价格计算。

[4] 国民总收入，原称国民生产总值，是指一个国家或地区所有常住单位在一定时期内所获得的初次分配收入总额，等于国内生产总值加上来自国外的初次分配收入净额。

[5] 万元国内生产总值能耗按2015年价格计算。

[6] 全员劳动生产率为国内生产总值（按2015年价格计算）与全部就业人员的比率。2020年就业人员数据为预计数。

图 2　2016–2020 年三次产业增加值占国内生产总值比重

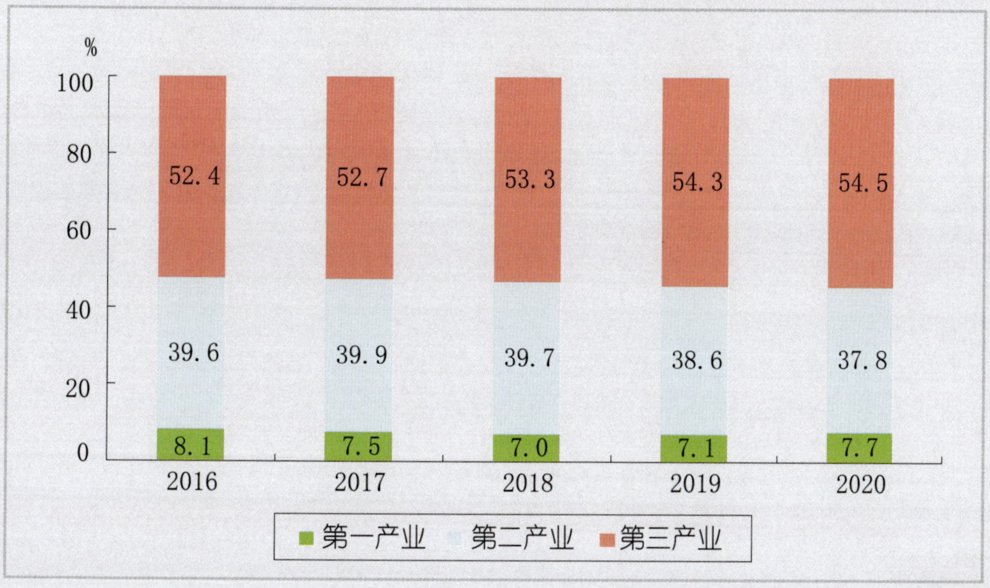

全年城镇新增就业 1186 万人，比上年少增 166 万人。年末全国城镇调查失业率为 5.2%，城镇登记失业率为 4.2%。全国农民工[7]总量 28560 万人，比上年下降 1.8%。其中，外出农民工 16959 万人，下降 2.7%；本地农民工 11601 万人，下降 0.4%。

图 3　2016–2020 年城镇新增就业人数

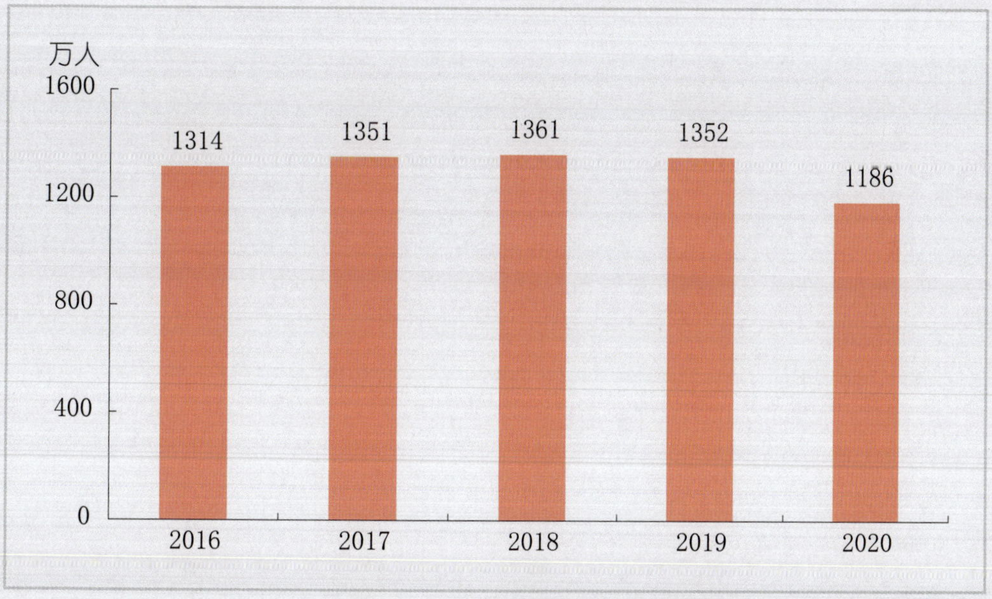

[7] 年度农民工数量包括年内在本乡镇以外从业 6 个月及以上的外出农民工和在本乡镇内从事非农产业 6 个月及以上的本地农民工。

全年居民消费价格比上年上涨2.5%。工业生产者出厂价格下降1.8%。工业生产者购进价格下降2.3%。农产品生产者价格[8]上涨15.0%。12月份，70个大中城市新建商品住宅销售价格同比上涨的城市个数为60个，下降的为10个。

图4　2020年居民消费价格月度涨跌幅度

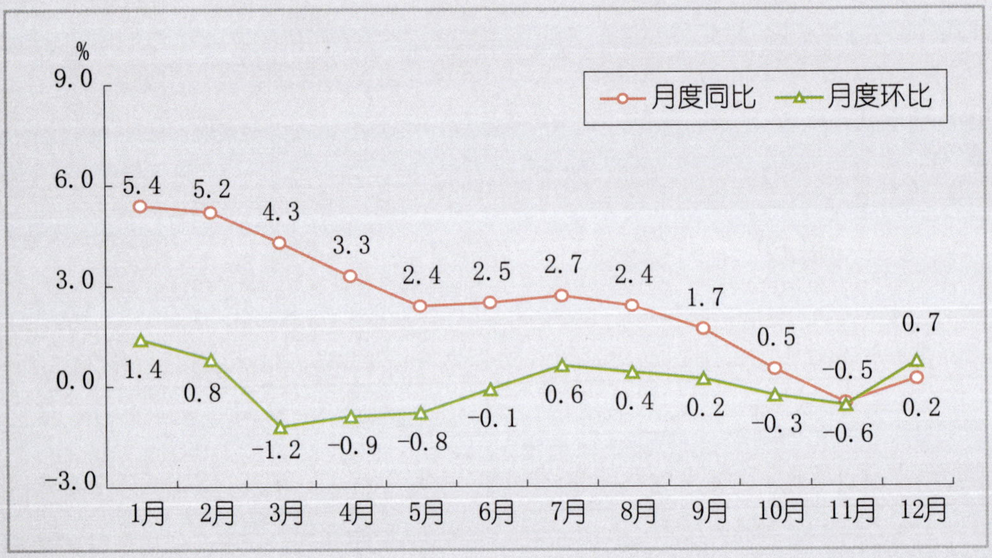

表1　2020年居民消费价格比上年涨跌幅度

单位：%

指　标	全　国	城　市	农　村
居民消费价格	2.5	2.3	3.0
其中：食品烟酒	8.3	7.8	9.6
衣　着	-0.2	-0.2	-0.3
居　住[9]	-0.4	-0.4	-0.5
生活用品及服务	0.0	0.1	-0.1
交通和通信	-3.5	-3.6	-3.2
教育文化和娱乐	1.3	1.4	1.1
医疗保健	1.8	1.7	2.0
其他用品和服务	4.3	4.4	4.1

[8] 农产品生产者价格是指农产品生产者直接出售其产品时的价格。
[9] 居住类价格包括租赁房房租、住房保养维修及管理、水电燃料等价格。

年末国家外汇储备32165亿美元，比上年末增加1086亿美元。全年人民币平均汇率为1美元兑6.8974元人民币，比上年升值0.02%。

图5 2016–2020年年末国家外汇储备

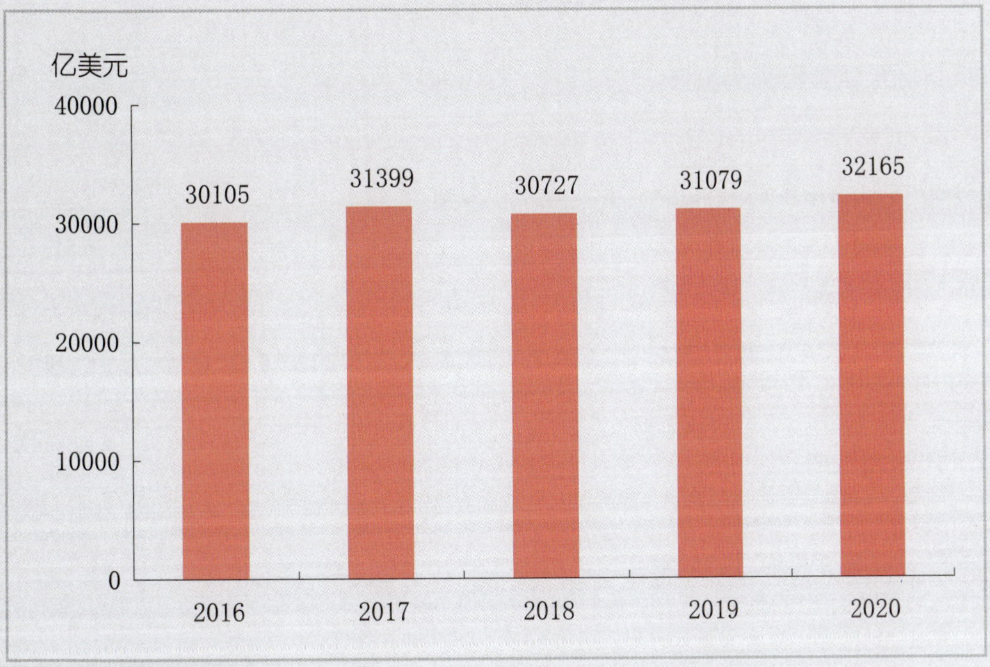

三大攻坚战取得决定性成就。按照每人每年生活水平2300元（2010年不变价）的现行农村贫困标准计算，551万农村贫困人口全部实现脱贫。党的十八大以来，9899万农村贫困人口全部实现脱贫，贫困县全部摘帽，绝对贫困历史性消除。全年贫困地区[10]农村居民人均可支配收入12588元，比上年增长8.8%，扣除价格因素，实际增长5.6%。在监测的337个地级及以上城市中，全年空气质量达标的城市占59.9%，未达标的城市占40.1%。细颗粒物（$PM_{2.5}$）未达标城市（基于2015年$PM_{2.5}$年平均浓度未达标的262个城市）年平均浓度37微克/立方米，比上年下降7.5%。1940个国家地表水考核断面中，全年水质优良（Ⅰ～Ⅲ类）断面比例为83.4%，Ⅳ类断面比例为13.6%，Ⅴ类断面比例为2.4%，劣Ⅴ类断面比例为0.6%。年末全国地方政府债务余额控制在全国人大批准的限额之内。金融风险处置取得重要阶段性成果。

[10] 贫困地区包括集中连片特困地区和片区外的国家扶贫开发工作重点县，原共有832个县。2017年开始将新疆阿克苏地区纳入贫困监测范围。

新产业新业态新模式逆势成长。全年规模以上工业中，高技术制造业[11]增加值比上年增长7.1%，占规模以上工业增加值的比重为15.1%；装备制造业[12]增加值增长6.6%，占规模以上工业增加值的比重为33.7%。全年规模以上服务业[13]中，战略性新兴服务业[14]企业营业收入比上年增长8.3%。全年高技术产业投资[15]比上年增长10.6%。全年新能源汽车产量145.6万辆，比上年增长17.3%；集成电路产量2614.7亿块，增长29.6%。全年网上零售额[16]117601亿元，按可比口径计算，比上年增长10.9%。全年新登记市场主体2502万户，日均新登记企业2.2万户，年末市场主体总数达1.4亿户。

城乡区域协调发展稳步推进。年末常住人口城镇化率超过60%。分区域看[17]，全年东部地区生产总值525752亿元，比上年增长2.9%；中部地区生产总值222246亿元，增长1.3%；西部地区生产总值213292亿元，增长3.3%；东北地区生产总值51125亿元，增长1.1%。全年京津冀地区生产总值86393亿元，比上年增长2.4%；长江经济带地区生产总值471580亿元，增长2.7%；长江三角洲地区生产总值244714亿元，增长3.3%。粤港澳大湾区建设、黄河流域生态保护和高质量发展等区域重大战略深入实施。

二、农业

全年粮食种植面积11677万公顷，比上年增加70万公顷。其中，稻谷种植面积3008万公顷，增加38万公顷；小麦种植面积2338万公顷，减少35万公顷；玉米种植面积4126万公顷，减少2万公顷。棉花种植面积317万公顷，减少17万公顷。油料种植面积1313万公顷，增加20万公顷。糖料种植面积157万公顷，减少4万公顷。

[11]高技术制造业包括医药制造业，航空、航天器及设备制造业，电子及通信设备制造业，计算机及办公设备制造业，医疗仪器设备及仪器仪表制造业，信息化学品制造业。

[12]装备制造业包括金属制品业，通用设备制造业，专用设备制造业，汽车制造业，铁路、船舶、航空航天和其他运输设备制造业，电气机械和器材制造业，计算机、通信和其他电子设备制造业，仪器仪表制造业。

[13]规模以上服务业统计范围包括：年营业收入2000万元及以上的交通运输、仓储和邮政业，信息传输、软件和信息技术服务业，水利、环境和公共设施管理业，卫生行业法人单位；年营业收入1000万元及以上的房地产业（不含房地产开发经营），租赁和商务服务业，科学研究和技术服务业，教育行业法人单位；以及年营业收入500万元及以上的居民服务、修理和其他服务业，文化、体育和娱乐业，社会工作行业法人单位。

[14]战略性新兴服务业包括新一代信息技术产业，高端装备制造产业，新材料产业，生物产业，新能源汽车产业，新能源产业，节能环保产业和数字创意产业等八大产业中的服务业相关行业，以及新技术与创新创业等相关服务业。2020年战略性新兴服务业企业营业收入增速按可比口径计算。

[15]高技术产业投资包括医药制造、航空航天器及设备制造等六大类高技术制造业投资和信息服务、电子商务服务等九大类高技术服务业投资。

[16]网上零售额是指通过公共网络交易平台（主要从事实物商品交易的网上平台，包括自建网站和第三方平台）实现的商品和服务零售额。

[17]东部地区是指北京、天津、河北、上海、江苏、浙江、福建、山东、广东和海南10省（市）；中部地区是指山西、安徽、江西、河南、湖北和湖南6省；西部地区是指内蒙古、广西、重庆、四川、贵州、云南、西藏、陕西、甘肃、青海、宁夏和新疆12省（区、市）；东北地区是指辽宁、吉林和黑龙江3省。

全年粮食产量 66949 万吨，比上年增加 565 万吨，增产 0.9%。其中，夏粮产量 14286 万吨，增产 0.9%；早稻产量 2729 万吨，增产 3.9%；秋粮产量 49934 万吨，增产 0.7%。全年谷物产量 61674 万吨，比上年增产 0.5%。其中，稻谷产量 21186 万吨，增产 1.1%；小麦产量 13425 万吨，增产 0.5%；玉米产量 26067 万吨，持平略减。

图 6　2016–2020 年粮食产量

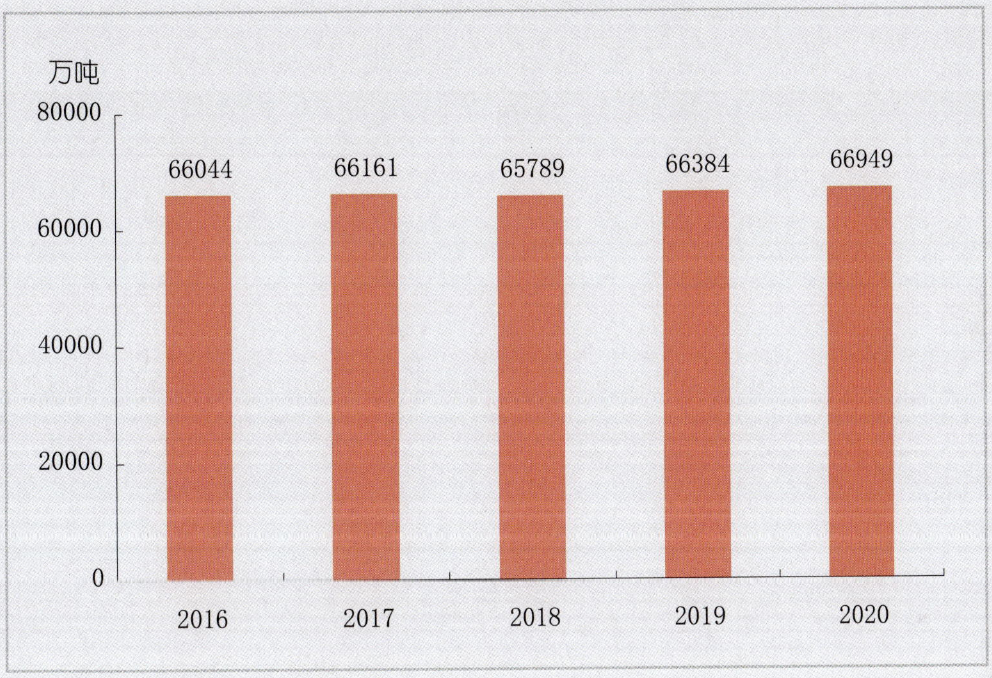

全年棉花产量 591 万吨，比上年增产 0.4%。油料产量 3585 万吨，增产 2.6%。糖料产量 12028 万吨，减产 1.2%。茶叶产量 297 万吨，增产 7.1%。

全年猪牛羊禽肉产量 7639 万吨，比上年下降 0.1%。其中，猪肉产量 4113 万吨，下降 3.3%；牛肉产量 672 万吨，增长 0.8%；羊肉产量 492 万吨，增长 1.0%；禽肉产量 2361 万吨，增长 5.5%。禽蛋产量 3468 万吨，增长 4.8%。牛奶产量 3440 万吨，增长 7.5%。年末生猪存栏 40650 万头，比上年末增长 31.0%；全年生猪出栏 52704 万头，比上年下降 3.2%。

全年水产品产量 6545 万吨，比上年增长 1.0%。其中，养殖水产品产量 5215 万吨，增长 3.0%；捕捞水产品产量 1330 万吨，下降 5.0%。

全年木材产量 8727 万立方米，比上年下降 13.1%。

全年新增耕地灌溉面积 43 万公顷，新增高效节水灌溉面积 160 万公顷。

三、工业和建筑业

全年全部工业增加值313071亿元，比上年增长2.4%。规模以上工业增加值增长2.8%。在规模以上工业中，分经济类型看，国有控股企业增加值增长2.2%；股份制企业增长3.0%，外商及港澳台商投资企业增长2.4%；私营企业增长3.7%。分门类看，采矿业增长0.5%，制造业增长3.4%，电力、热力、燃气及水生产和供应业增长2.0%。

图7　2016—2020年全部工业增加值及其增长速度

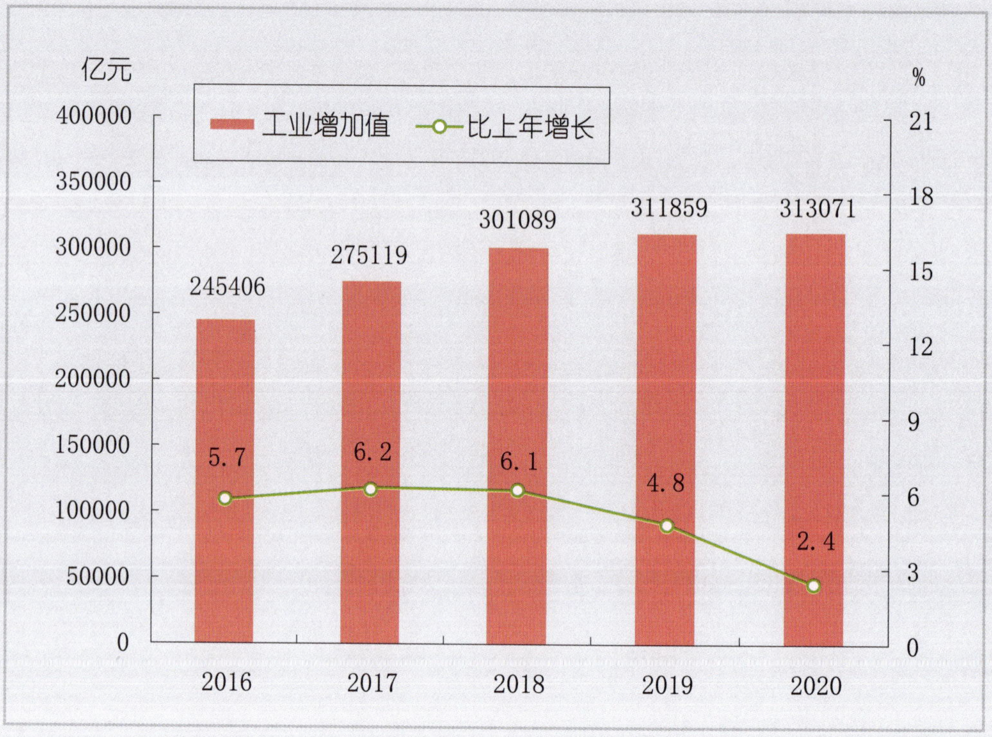

全年规模以上工业中，农副食品加工业增加值比上年下降1.5%，纺织业增长0.7%，化学原料和化学制品制造业增长3.4%，非金属矿物制品业增长2.8%，黑色金属冶炼和压延加工业增长6.7%，通用设备制造业增长5.1%，专用设备制造业增长6.3%，汽车制造业增长6.6%，电气机械和器材制造业增长8.9%，计算机、通信和其他电子设备制造业增长7.7%，电力、热力生产和供应业增长1.9%。

表 2 2020 年主要工业产品产量及其增长速度[18]

产品名称	单位	产量	比上年增长（%）
纱	万吨	2618.3	-7.4
布	亿米	460.3	-17.1
化学纤维	万吨	6126.5	4.1
成品糖	万吨	1431.3	3.0
卷烟	亿支	23863.7	0.9
彩色电视机	万台	19626.2	3.3
其中：液晶电视机	万台	19247.2	3.0
家用电冰箱	万台	9014.7	14.0
房间空气调节器	万台	21035.3	-3.8
一次能源生产总量	亿吨标准煤	40.8	2.8
原煤	亿吨	39.0	1.4
原油	万吨	19476.9	1.6
天然气	亿立方米	1925.0	9.8
发电量	亿千瓦小时	77790.6	3.7
其中：火电[19]	亿千瓦小时	53302.5	2.1
水电	亿千瓦小时	13552.1	3.9
核电	亿千瓦小时	3662.5	5.1
粗钢	万吨	106476.7	7.0
钢材[20]	万吨	132489.2	10.0
十种有色金属	万吨	6188.4	5.5
其中：精炼铜（电解铜）	万吨	1002.5	2.5
原　铝（电解铝）	万吨	3708.0	5.6
水泥	亿吨	24.0	2.5
硫酸（折 100%）	万吨	9238.2	1.3
烧碱（折 100%）	万吨	3673.9	6.2
乙烯	万吨	2160.0	5.2
化肥（折 100%）	万吨	5496.0	-4.1
发电机组（发电设备）	万千瓦	13226.2	38.3
汽车	万辆	2532.5	-1.4
其中：基本型乘用车（轿车）	万辆	923.9	-10.2
运动型多用途乘用车（SUV）	万辆	905.0	2.6
大中型拖拉机	万台	34.6	23.0
集成电路	亿块	2614.7	29.6
程控交换机	万线	702.5	-11.1
移动通信手持机	万台	146961.8	-13.3
微型计算机设备	万台	37800.4	10.6
工业机器人	万台（套）	21.2	20.7

[18] 2019 年部分产品产量数据进行了核实调整，2020 年产量增速按可比口径计算。

[19] 火电包括燃煤发电量，燃油发电量，燃气发电量，余热、余压、余气发电量，垃圾焚烧发电量，生物质发电量。

[20] 钢材产量数据中含企业之间重复加工钢材约 30566 万吨。

年末全国发电装机容量220058万千瓦，比上年末增长9.5%。其中[21]，火电装机容量124517万千瓦，增长4.7%；水电装机容量37016万千瓦，增长3.4%；核电装机容量4989万千瓦，增长2.4%；并网风电装机容量28153万千瓦，增长34.6%；并网太阳能发电装机容量25343万千瓦，增长24.1%。

全年规模以上工业企业利润64516亿元，比上年增长4.1%[22]。分经济类型看，国有控股企业利润14861亿元，比上年下降2.9%；股份制企业45445亿元，增长3.4%，外商及港澳台商投资企业18234亿元，增长7.0%；私营企业20262亿元，增长3.1%。分门类看，采矿业利润3553亿元，比上年下降31.5%；制造业55795亿元，增长7.6%；电力、热力、燃气及水生产和供应业5168亿元，增长4.9%。全年规模以上工业企业每百元营业收入中的成本为83.89元，比上年减少0.11元；营业收入利润率为6.08%，提高0.20个百分点。年末规模以上工业企业资产负债率为56.1%，比上年末下降0.3个百分点。全年全国工业产能利用率[23]为74.5%，其中一、二、三、四季度分别为67.3%、74.4%、76.7%、78.0%。

全年全社会建筑业增加值72996亿元，比上年增长3.5%。全国具有资质等级的总承包和专业承包建筑业企业利润8303亿元，比上年增长0.3%，其中国有控股企业2871亿元，增长4.7%。

图8　2016—2020年建筑业增加值及其增长速度

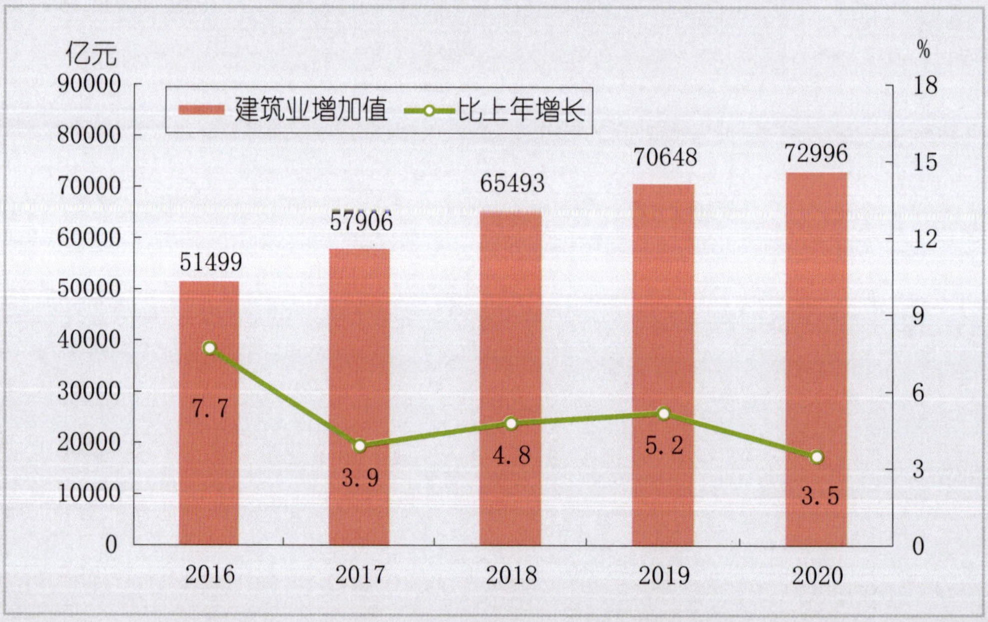

[21] 少量发电装机容量（如地热等）公报中未列出。

[22] 由于统计调查制度规定的口径调整、统计执法、剔除重复数据等因素，2020年规模以上工业企业财务指标增速及变化按可比口径计算。

[23] 产能利用率是指实际产出与生产能力（均以价值量计量）的比率。企业的实际产出是指企业报告期内的工业总产值；企业的生产能力是指报告期内，在劳动力、原材料、燃料、运输等保证供给的情况下，生产设备（机械）保持正常运行，企业可实现并能长期维持的产品产出。

四、服务业

全年批发和零售业增加值 95686 亿元，比上年下降 1.3%；交通运输、仓储和邮政业增加值 41562 亿元，增长 0.5%；住宿和餐饮业增加值 15971 亿元，下降 13.1%；金融业增加值 84070 亿元，增长 7.0%；房地产业增加值 74553 亿元，增长 2.9%；信息传输、软件和信息技术服务业增加值 37951 亿元，增长 16.9%；租赁和商务服务业增加值 31616 亿元，下降 5.3%。全年规模以上服务业企业营业收入比上年增长 1.9%，利润总额下降 7.0%。

图 9　2016–2020 年服务业增加值及其增长速度

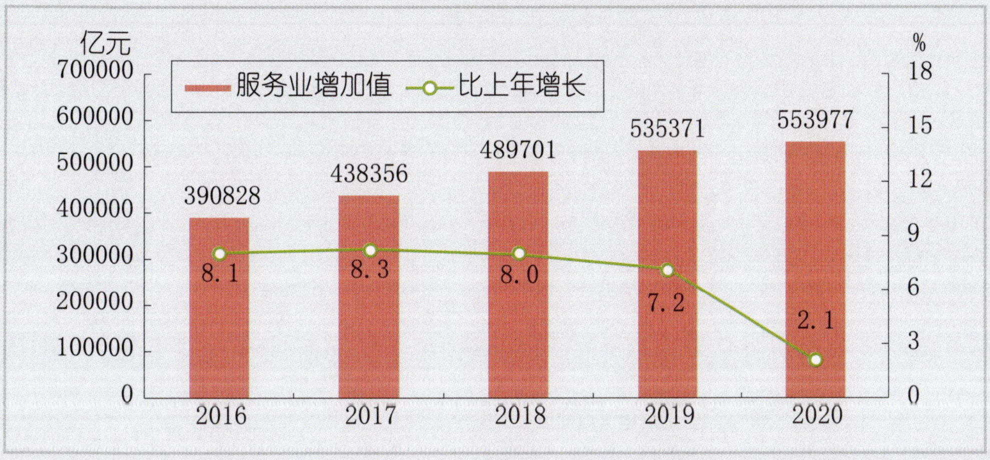

全年货物运输总量[24]463 亿吨，货物运输周转量 196618 亿吨公里。全年港口完成货物吞吐量 145 亿吨，比上年增长 4.3%，其中外贸货物吞吐量 45 亿吨，增长 4.0%。港口集装箱吞吐量 26430 万标准箱，增长 1.2%。

表 3　2020 年各种运输方式完成货物运输量及其增长速度

指　标	单　位	绝对数	比上年增长（%）
货物运输总量	**亿吨**	**463.4**	**-0.5**
铁路	亿吨	44.6	3.2
公路	亿吨	342.6	-0.3
水运	亿吨	76.2	-3.3
民航	万吨	676.6	-10.2
货物运输周转量	**亿吨公里**	**196618.3**	**-1.0**
铁路	亿吨公里	30371.8	1.0
公路	亿吨公里	60171.8	0.9
水运	亿吨公里	105834.4	-2.5
民航	亿吨公里	240.2	-8.7

[24] 货物运输总量及周转量包括铁路、公路、水路和民航四种运输方式完成量，2020 年增速按可比口径计算。因新组建国家管网集团，部分油气运输管线统计归口发生变化等原因，管道运输相关数据尚在核实。

全年旅客运输总量97亿人次，比上年下降45.1%。旅客运输周转量19251亿人公里，下降45.5%。

表4　2020年各种运输方式完成旅客运输量及其增长速度

指　标	单　位	绝对数	比上年增长（%）
旅客运输总量	**亿人次**	**96.7**	**-45.1**
铁路	亿人次	22.0	-39.8
公路	亿人次	68.9	-47.0
水运	亿人次	1.5	-45.2
民航	亿人次	4.2	-36.7
旅客运输周转量	**亿人公里**	**19251.4**	**-45.5**
铁路	亿人公里	8266.2	-43.8
公路	亿人公里	4641.0	-47.6
水运	亿人公里	33.0	-58.0
民航	亿人公里	6311.2	-46.1

年末全国民用汽车保有量28087万辆（包括三轮汽车和低速货车748万辆），比上年末增加1937万辆，其中私人汽车保有量24393万辆，增加1758万辆。民用轿车保有量15640万辆，增加996万辆，其中私人轿车保有量14674万辆，增加973万辆。

全年完成邮政行业业务总量[25]21053亿元，比上年增长29.7%。邮政业全年完成邮政函件业务14.2亿件，包裹业务0.2亿件，快递业务量833.6亿件，快递业务收入8795亿元。全年完成电信业务总量[26]136758亿元，比上年增长28.1%。年末全国电话用户总数177598万户，其中移动电话用户159407万户。移动电话普及率为113.9部/百人。固定互联网宽带接入用户[27]48355万户，比上年末增加3427万户，其中固定互联网光纤宽带接入用户[28]45414万户，增加3675万户。全年移动互联网用户接入流量1656亿GB，比上年增长35.7%。年末互联网上网人数9.89亿人，其中手机上网人数[29]9.86亿人。互联网普及率为70.4%，其中农村地区互联网普及率为55.9%。全年软件和信息技术服务业[30]完成软件业务收入81616亿元，按可比口径计算，比上年增长13.3%。

---

[25]邮政行业业务总量按2010年价格计算。

[26]电信业务总量按2015年价格计算。

[27]固定互联网宽带接入用户是指报告期末在电信企业登记注册，通过xDSL、FTTx+LAN、FTTH/O以及其他宽带接入方式和普通专线接入公众互联网的用户。

[28]固定互联网光纤宽带接入用户是指报告期末在电信企业登记注册，通过FTTH或FTTO方式接入公众互联网的用户。

[29]手机上网人数是指过去半年通过手机接入并使用互联网的人数。

[30]软件和信息技术服务业包括软件开发，集成电路设计，信息系统集成和物联网技术服务，运行维护服务，信息处理和存储支持服务，信息技术咨询服务，数字内容服务和其他信息技术服务等行业。

图 10　2016—2020 年快递业务量及其增长速度

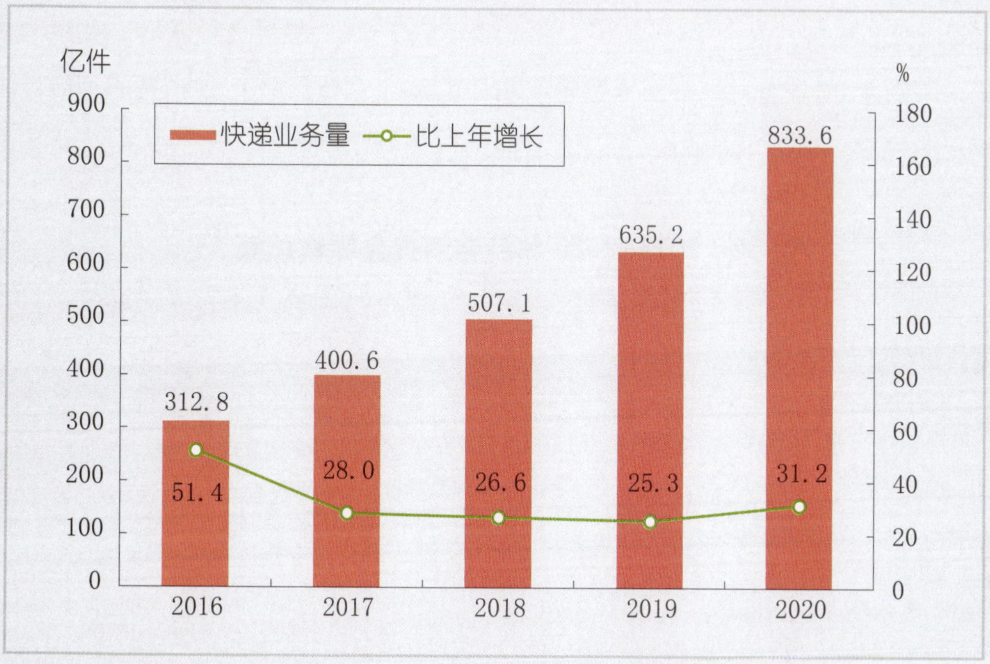

图 11　2016—2020 年年末固定互联网宽带接入用户数

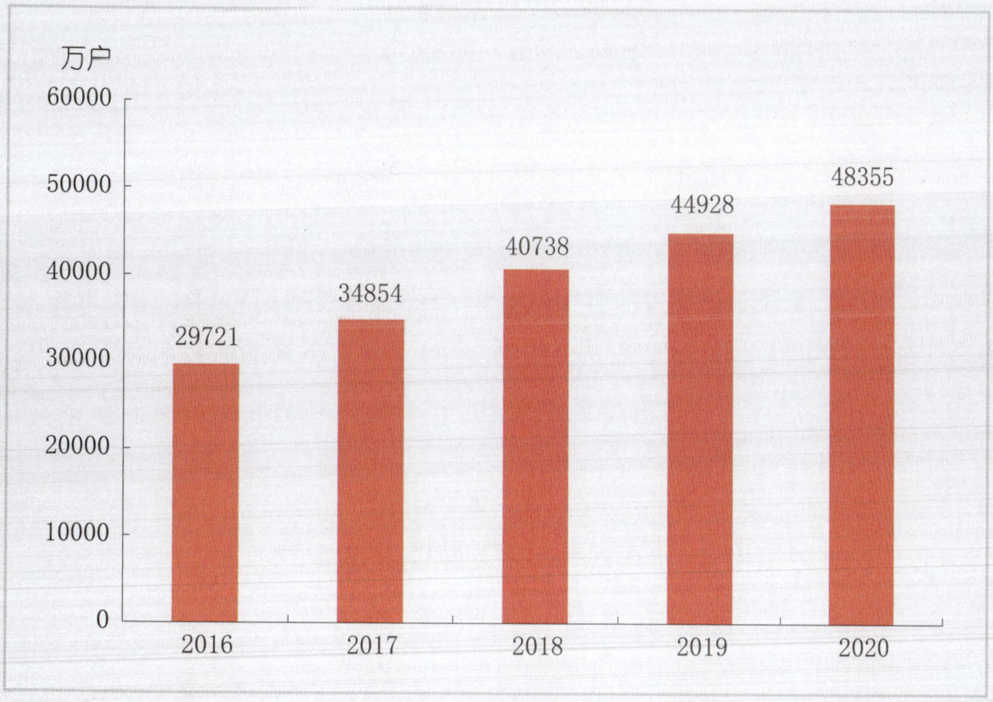

五、国内贸易

全年社会消费品零售总额391981亿元，比上年下降3.9%。按经营地统计，城镇消费品零售额339119亿元，下降4.0%；乡村消费品零售额52862亿元，下降3.2%。按消费类型统计，商品零售额352453亿元，下降2.3%；餐饮收入额39527亿元，下降16.6%。

图12 2016-2020年社会消费品零售总额[31]

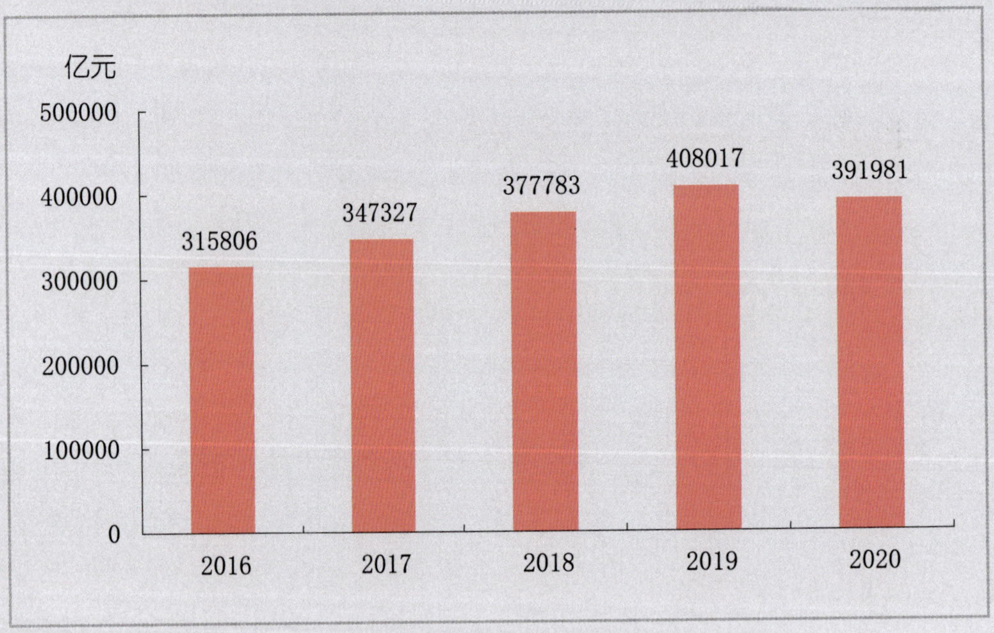

全年限额以上单位商品零售额中，粮油、食品类零售额比上年增长9.9%，饮料类增长14.0%，烟酒类增长5.4%，服装、鞋帽、针纺织品类下降6.6%，化妆品类增长9.5%，金银珠宝类下降4.7%，日用品类增长7.5%，家用电器和音像器材类下降3.8%，中西药品类增长7.8%，文化办公用品类增长5.8%，家具类下降7.0%，通讯器材类增长12.9%，建筑及装潢材料类下降2.8%，石油及制品类下降14.5%，汽车类下降1.8%。

全年实物商品网上零售额97590亿元，按可比口径计算，比上年增长14.8%，占社会消费品零售总额的比重为24.9%，比上年提高4.0个百分点。

[31]根据第四次全国经济普查结果及有关制度规定，对2016—2019年社会消费品零售总额数据进行了修订。

六、固定资产投资

全年全社会固定资产投资[32]527270 亿元，比上年增长 2.7%。其中，固定资产投资（不含农户）518907 亿元，增长 2.9%。分区域看[33]，东部地区投资比上年增长 3.8%，中部地区投资增长 0.7%，西部地区投资增长 4.4%，东北地区投资增长 4.3%。

在固定资产投资（不含农户）中，第一产业投资 13302 亿元，比上年增长 19.5%；第二产业投资 149154 亿元，增长 0.1%；第三产业投资 356451 亿元，增长 3.6%。民间固定资产投资[34]289264 亿元，增长 1.0%。基础设施投资[35]增长 0.9%。

图 13　2020 年三次产业投资占固定资产投资（不含农户）比重

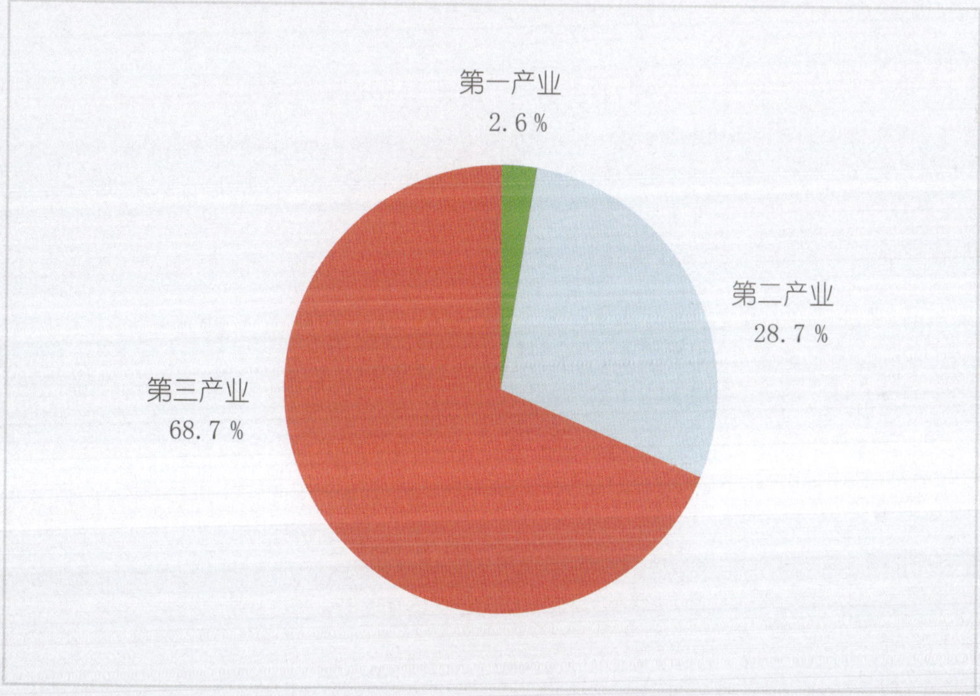

[32] 根据第四次全国经济普查、统计执法检查、统计调查方法改革和制度规定，对 2019 年固定资产投资数据进行修订，2020 年增速按可比口径计算。

[33] 见注释 [17]。

[34] 民间固定资产投资是指具有集体、私营、个人性质的内资调查单位以及由其控股（包括绝对控股和相对控股）的调查单位建造或购置固定资产的投资。

[35] 基础设施投资包括交通运输、邮政业，电信、广播电视和卫星传输服务业，互联网和相关服务业，水利、环境和公共设施管理业投资。

表5 2020年分行业固定资产投资（不含农户）增长速度

行　业	比上年增长（%）	行　业	比上年增长（%）
总　计	2.9	金融业	-13.3
农、林、牧、渔业	19.1	房地产业[36]	5.0
采矿业	-14.1	租赁和商务服务业	5.0
制造业	-2.2	科学研究和技术服务业	3.4
电力、热力、燃气及水生产和供应业	17.6	水利、环境和公共设施管理业	0.2
建筑业	9.2	居民服务、修理和其他服务业	-2.9
批发和零售业	-21.5	教育	12.3
交通运输、仓储和邮政业	1.4	卫生和社会工作	26.8
住宿和餐饮业	-5.5	文化、体育和娱乐业	1.0
信息传输、软件和信息技术服务业	18.7	公共管理、社会保障和社会组织	-6.4

表6 2020年固定资产投资新增主要生产与运营能力

指　标	单　位	绝对数
新增220千伏及以上变电设备	万千伏安	22288
新建铁路投产里程	公里	4933
其中：高速铁路	公里	2521
增、新建铁路复线投产里程	公里	3380
电气化铁路投产里程	公里	5480
新改建高速公路里程	公里	12713
港口万吨级码头泊位新增通过能力	万吨/年	30562
新增民用运输机场	个	3
新增光缆线路长度	万公里	428

[36] 房地产业投资除房地产开发投资外，还包括建设单位自建房屋以及物业管理、中介服务和其他房地产投资。

全年房地产开发投资141443亿元，比上年增长7.0%。其中住宅投资104446亿元，增长7.6%；办公楼投资6494亿元，增长5.4%；商业营业用房投资13076亿元，下降1.1%。年末商品房待售面积49850万平方米，比上年末增加29万平方米。其中，商品住宅待售面积22379万平方米，减少94万平方米。

全年全国各类棚户区改造开工209万套，基本建成203万套。全面完成74.21万户[37]建档立卡贫困户脱贫攻坚农村危房改造扫尾工程任务。

表7　2020年房地产开发和销售主要指标及其增长速度

指　标	单　位	绝对数	比上年增长（%）
投资额	亿元	141443	7.0
其中：住宅	亿元	104446	7.6
房屋施工面积	万平方米	926759	3.7
其中：住宅	万平方米	655558	4.4
房屋新开工面积	万平方米	224433	-1.2
其中：住宅	万平方米	164329	-1.9
房屋竣工面积	万平方米	91218	-4.9
其中：住宅	万平方米	65910	-3.1
商品房销售面积	万平方米	176086	2.6
其中：住宅	万平方米	154878	3.2
本年到位资金	亿元	193115	8.1
其中：国内贷款	亿元	26676	5.7
个人按揭贷款	亿元	29976	9.9

七、对外经济

全年货物进出口总额321557亿元，比上年增长1.9%。其中，出口179326亿元，增长4.0%；进口142231亿元，下降0.7%。货物进出口顺差37096亿元，比上年增加7976亿元。对“一带一路”[38]沿线国家进出口总额93696亿元，比上年增长1.0%。其中，出口54263亿元，增长3.2%；进口39433亿元，下降1.8%。

[37] 数据包括2019年全国64.16万户建档立卡贫困户存量危房和脱贫攻坚“回头看”排查新增的10.05万户建档立卡贫困户危房。

[38] “一带一路”是指“丝绸之路经济带”和“21世纪海上丝绸之路”。

图 14 2016–2020 年货物进出口总额

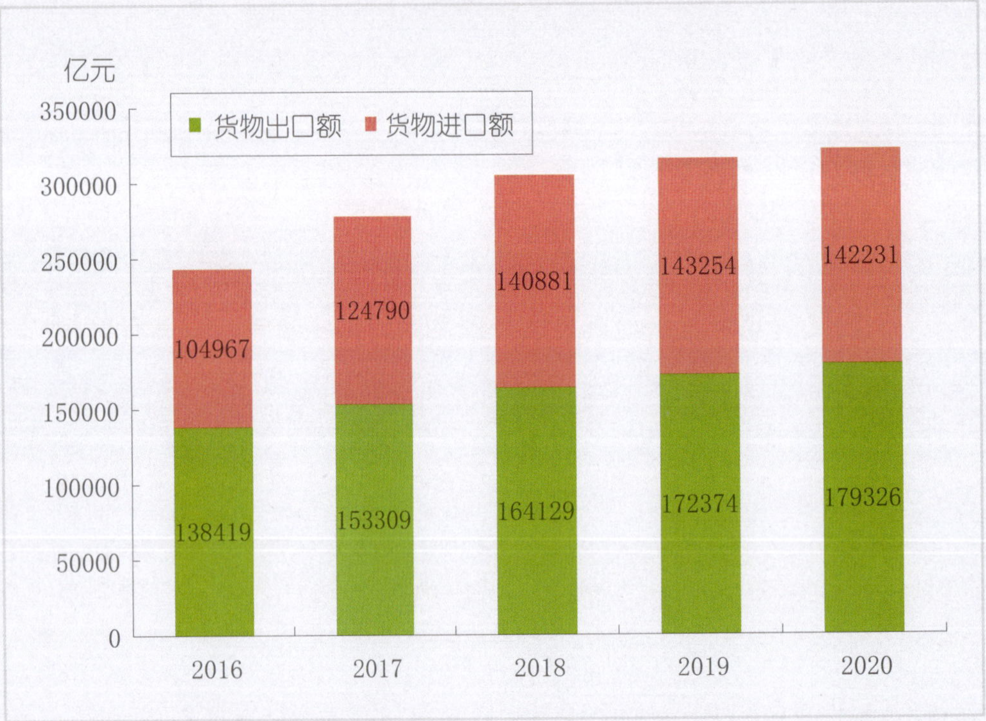

表 8 2020 年货物进出口总额及其增长速度

指 标	金额（亿元）	比上年增长（%）
货物进出口总额	321557	1.9
货物出口额	179326	4.0
其中：一般贸易	106460	6.9
加工贸易	48589	-4.2
其中：机电产品	106608	6.0
高新技术产品	53692	6.5
货物进口额	142231	-0.7
其中：一般贸易	86048	-0.7
加工贸易	27853	-3.2
其中：机电产品	65625	4.8
高新技术产品	47160	7.2
货物进出口顺差	37096	—

表 9　2020 年主要商品出口数量、金额及其增长速度

商品名称	单　位	数　量	比上年增长（%）	金　额（亿元）	比上年增长（%）
钢材	万吨	5367	-16.5	3151	-14.8
纺织纱线、织物及制品	—	—	—	10695	30.4
服装及衣着附件	—	—	—	9520	-6.0
鞋靴	万双	740137	-22.4	2454	-20.9
家具及其零件	—	—	—	4039	12.2
箱包及类似容器	万吨	201	-34.7	1429	-23.9
玩具	—	—	—	2317	7.7
塑料制品	—	—	—	5902	20.0
集成电路	亿个	2598	18.8	8056	15.0
自动数据处理设备及其零部件	—	—	—	14599	12.0
手机	万台	96640	-2.8	8647	0.4
集装箱	万个	198	-17.9	508	10.5
液晶显示板	万个	126747	-15.9	1370	-7.1
汽车（包括底盘）	万辆	108	-13.2	1090	-3.2

表 10　2020 年主要商品进口数量、金额及其增长速度

商品名称	单　位	数　量	比上年增长（%）	金　额（亿元）	比上年增长（%）
大豆	万吨	10033	13.3	2743	12.5
食用植物油	万吨	983	3.1	515	17.7
铁矿砂及其精矿	万吨	117010	9.5	8229	17.8
煤及褐煤	万吨	30399	1.5	1411	-12.1
原油	万吨	54239	7.3	12218	-26.8
成品油	万吨	2835	-7.2	818	-30.4
天然气	万吨	10166	5.3	2315	-19.4
初级形状的塑料	万吨	4063	10.1	3628	-1.2
纸浆	万吨	3063	12.7	1088	-7.6
钢材	万吨	2023	64.4	1165	19.8
未锻轧铜及铜材	万吨	668	34.1	2988	33.4
集成电路	亿个	5435	22.1	24207	14.8
汽车（包括底盘）	万辆	93	-11.4	3242	-3.5

表11 2020年对主要国家和地区货物进出口金额、增长速度及其比重

国家和地区	出口额（亿元）	比上年增长（%）	占全部出口比重（%）	进口额（亿元）	比上年增长（%）	占全部进口比重（%）
东盟	26550	7.0	14.8	20807	6.9	14.6
欧盟[39]	27084	7.2	15.1	17874	2.6	12.6
美国	31279	8.4	17.4	9319	10.1	6.6
日本	9883	0.1	5.5	12090	2.1	8.5
韩国	7787	1.8	4.3	11957	0.0	8.4
中国香港	18830	-2.2	10.5	482	-22.9	0.3
中国台湾	4163	9.5	2.3	13873	16.2	9.8
巴西	2417	-1.5	1.3	5834	5.8	4.1
俄罗斯	3506	2.1	2.0	3960	-6.1	2.8
印度	4613	-10.5	2.6	1445	16.7	1.0
南非	1055	-7.5	0.6	1422	-20.4	1.0

全年服务进出口总额45643亿元，比上年下降15.7%。其中，服务出口19357亿元，下降1.1%；服务进口26286亿元，下降24.0%。服务进出口逆差6929亿元。

全年外商直接投资（不含银行、证券、保险领域）新设立企业38570家，比上年下降5.7%。实际使用外商直接投资金额10000亿元，增长6.2%，折1444亿美元，增长4.5%。其中“一带一路”沿线国家对华直接投资（含通过部分自由港对华投资）新设立企业4294家，下降23.2%；对华直接投资金额574亿元，下降0.3%，折83亿美元，下降1.8%。全年高技术产业实际使用外资2963亿元，增长11.4%，折428亿美元，增长9.5%。

表12 2020年外商直接投资（不含银行、证券、保险领域）及其增长速度

行业	企业数（家）	比上年增长（%）	实际使用金额（亿元）	比上年增长（%）
总计	38570	-5.7	10000	6.2
其中：农、林、牧、渔业	493	-0.4	40	4.9
制造业	3732	-30.8	2156	-10.8
电力、热力、燃气及水生产和供应业	260	-11.9	217	-9.4
交通运输、仓储和邮政业	592	0.2	347	12.1
信息传输、软件和信息技术服务业	3521	-18.0	1133	13.3
批发和零售业	10812	-21.9	819	33.3
房地产业	1190	13.3	1407	-12.5
租赁和商务服务业	7513	30.1	1838	22.6
居民服务、修理和其他服务业	447	23.8	21	-42.4

[39] 对欧盟的货物进出口金额不包括英国数据，增速按可比口径计算。

全年对外非金融类直接投资额7598亿元，比上年下降0.4%，折1102亿美元，下降0.4%。其中，对“一带一路”沿线国家非金融类直接投资额178亿美元，增长18.3%。

表 13　2020 年对外非金融类直接投资额及其增长速度

行　业	金额（亿美元）	比上年增长（%）
总　计	1101.5	-0.4
其中：农、林、牧、渔业	13.9	-9.7
采矿业	50.9	-32.3
制造业	199.7	-0.5
电力、热力、燃气及水生产和供应业	27.8	10.3
建筑业	51.6	-39.4
批发和零售业	160.7	27.8
交通运输、仓储和邮政业	26.5	-52.3
信息传输、软件和信息技术服务业	67.1	9.6
房地产业	27.3	-43.4
租赁和商务服务业	417.9	17.5

全年对外承包工程完成营业额10756亿元，比上年下降9.8%，折1559亿美元，下降9.8%。其中，对“一带一路”沿线国家完成营业额911亿美元，下降7.0%，占对外承包工程完成营业额比重为58.4%。对外劳务合作派出各类劳务人员30万人。

八、财政金融

全年全国一般公共预算收入182895亿元，比上年下降3.9%。其中税收收入154310亿元，下降2.3%。全国一般公共预算支出245588亿元，比上年增长2.8%。全年新增减税降费超过2.5万亿元。

图 15　2016-2020 年全国一般公共预算收入

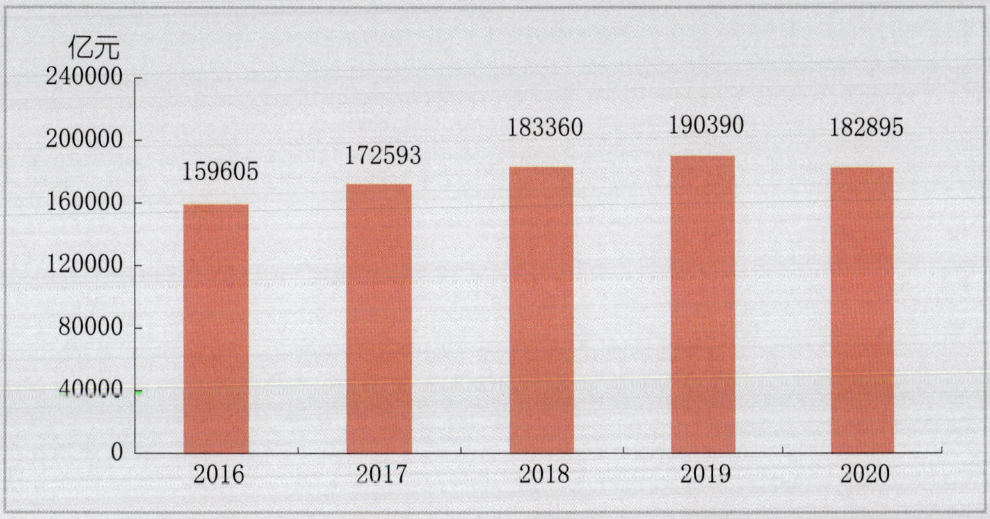

注：图中2016年至2019年数据为全国一般公共预算收入决算数，2020年为执行数。

年末广义货币供应量（M_2）余额218.7万亿元，比上年末增长10.1%；狭义货币供应量（M_1）余额62.6万亿元，增长8.6%；流通中货币（M_0）余额8.4万亿元，增长9.2%。

全年社会融资规模增量[40]34.9万亿元，按可比口径计算，比上年多9.2万亿元；年末社会融资规模存量[41]284.8万亿元，按可比口径计算，比上年末增长13.3%，其中对实体经济发放的人民币贷款余额171.6万亿元，增长13.2%。年末全部金融机构本外币各项存款余额218.4万亿元，比年初增加20.2万亿元，其中人民币各项存款余额212.6万亿元，增加19.6万亿元。全部金融机构本外币各项贷款余额178.4万亿元，增加19.8万亿元，其中人民币各项贷款余额172.7万亿元，增加19.6万亿元。人民币普惠金融贷款[42]余额21.5万亿元，增加4.2万亿元。

表14　2020年年末全部金融机构本外币存贷款余额及其增长速度

指　标	年末数（亿元）	比上年末增长（%）
各项存款	**2183744**	**10.2**
其中：境内住户存款	934383	13.8
其中：人民币	925986	13.9
境内非金融企业存款	688218	10.8
各项贷款	**1784034**	**12.5**
其中：境内短期贷款	492682	4.3
境内中长期贷款	1137504	17.1

年末主要农村金融机构（农村信用社、农村合作银行、农村商业银行）人民币贷款余额215886亿元，比年初增加25210亿元。全部金融机构人民币消费贷款余额495668亿元，增加55994亿元。其中，个人短期消费贷款余额87774亿元，增加7177亿元；个人中长期消费贷款余额407894亿元，增加48817亿元。

[40]社会融资规模增量是指一定时期内实体经济从金融体系获得的资金总额。

[41]社会融资规模存量是指一定时期末（月末、季末或年末）实体经济（境内非金融企业和个人）从金融体系获得的资金余额。

[42]普惠金融贷款包括单户授信小于1000万元的小微型企业贷款、个体工商户经营性贷款、小微企业主经营性贷款、农户生产经营贷款、建档立卡贫困人口消费贷款、创业担保贷款和助学贷款。

全年沪深交易所 A 股累计筹资[43]15417 亿元，比上年增加 1883 亿元。首次公开发行上市 A 股 394 只，筹资 4742 亿元，比上年增加 2252 亿元，其中科创板股票 145 只，筹资 2226 亿元；A 股再融资（包括公开增发、定向增发、配股、优先股、可转债转股）10674 亿元，减少 370 亿元。全年各类主体通过沪深交易所发行债券（包括公司债、可转债、可交换债、政策性金融债、地方政府债和企业资产支持证券）筹资 84777 亿元，比上年增加 12791 亿元。全国中小企业股份转让系统[44]挂牌公司 8187 家，全年挂牌公司累计股票筹资 339 亿元。

全年发行公司信用类债券[45]14.2 万亿元，比上年增加 3.5 万亿元。

全年保险公司原保险保费收入[46]45257 亿元，比上年增长 6.1%。其中，寿险业务原保险保费收入 23982 亿元，健康险和意外伤害险业务原保险保费收入 9347 亿元，财产险业务原保险保费收入 11929 亿元。支付各类赔款及给付 13907 亿元。其中，寿险业务给付 3715 亿元，健康险和意外伤害险业务赔款及给付 3237 亿元，财产险业务赔款 6955 亿元。

九、居民收入消费和社会保障

全年全国居民人均可支配收入 32189 元，比上年增长 4.7%，扣除价格因素，实际增长 2.1%。全国居民人均可支配收入中位数[47]27540 元，增长 3.8%。按常住地分，城镇居民人均可支配收入 43834 元，比上年增长 3.5%，扣除价格因素，实际增长 1.2%。城镇居民人均可支配收入中位数 40378 元，增长 2.9%。农村居民人均可支配收入 17131 元，比上年增长 6.9%，扣除价格因素，实际增长 3.8%。农村居民人均可支配收入中位数 15204 元，增长 5.7%。城乡居民人均可支配收入比值为 2.56，比上年缩小 0.08。按全国居民五等份收入分组[48]，低收入组人均可支配收入 7869 元，中间偏下收入组人均可支配收入 16443 元，中间收入组人均可支配收入 26249 元，中间偏上收入组人均可支配收入 41172 元，高收入组人均可支配收入 80294 元。全国农民工人均月收入 4072 元，比上年增长 2.8%。

[43] 沪深交易所股票筹资额按上市日统计，筹资额包括了可转债实际转股金额，2019 年、2020 年可转债实际转股金额分别为 995 亿元和 1195 亿元。

[44] 全国中小企业股份转让系统又称“新三板”，是 2012 年经国务院批准的全国性证券交易场所。全年全国中小企业股份转让系统挂牌公司累计筹资不含优先股，股票筹资按发行报告书的披露日统计。

[45] 公司信用类债券包括非金融企业债务融资工具、企业债券以及公司债、可转债等。

[46] 原保险保费收入是指保险企业确认的原保险合同保费收入。

[47] 人均收入中位数是指将所有调查户按人均收入水平从低到高（或从高到低）顺序排列，处于最中间位置调查户的人均收入。

[48] 全国居民五等份收入分组是指将所有调查户按人均收入水平从低到高顺序排列，平均分为五个等份，处于最低 20% 的收入家庭为低收入组，依此类推依次为中间偏下收入组、中间收入组、中间偏上收入组、高收入组。

全年全国居民人均消费支出21210元，比上年下降1.6%，扣除价格因素，实际下降4.0%。其中，人均服务性消费支出[49]9037元，比上年下降8.6%，占居民人均消费支出的比重为42.6%。按常住地分，城镇居民人均消费支出27007元，下降3.8%，扣除价格因素，实际下降6.0%；农村居民人均消费支出13713元，增长2.9%，扣除价格因素，实际下降0.1%。全国居民恩格尔系数为30.2%，其中城镇为29.2%，农村为32.7%。

图16 2016–2020年全国居民人均可支配收入及其增长速度

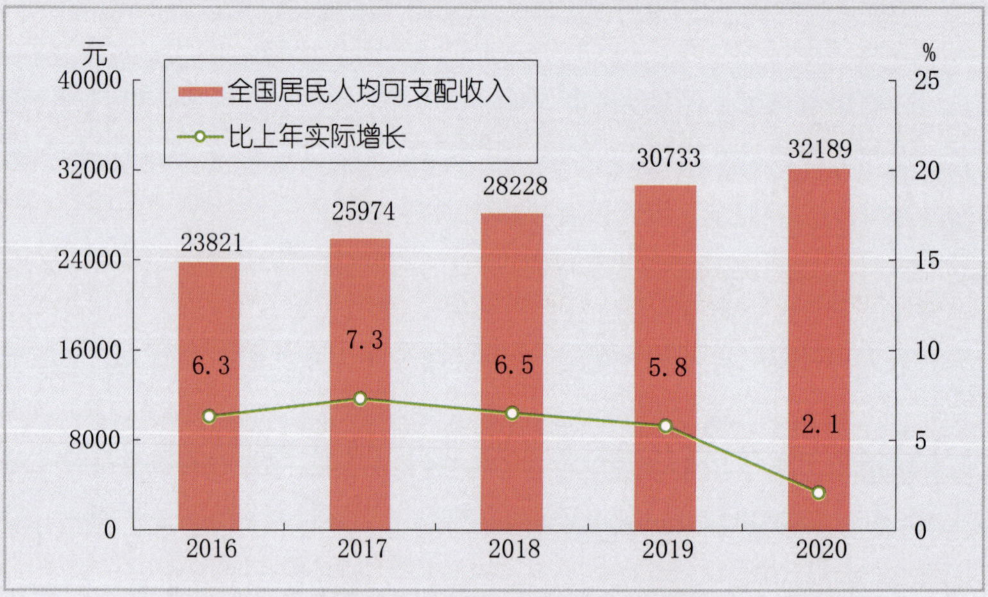

图17 2020年全国居民人均消费支出及其构成

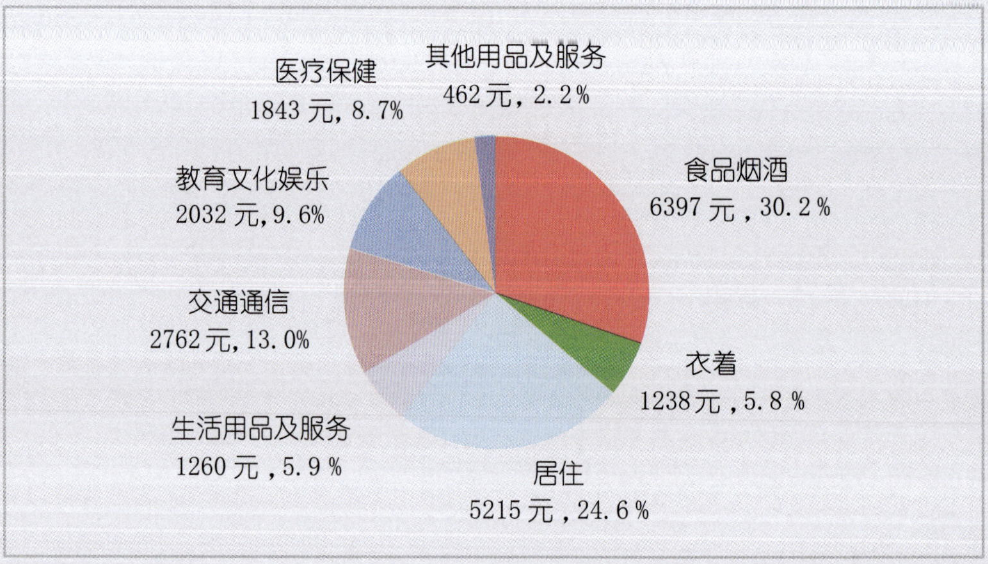

[49]服务性消费支出是指住户用于餐饮服务、教育文化娱乐服务和医疗服务等各种生活服务的消费支出。

年末全国参加城镇职工基本养老保险人数45638万人，比上年末增加2150万人。参加城乡居民基本养老保险人数54244万人，增加978万人。参加基本医疗保险人数136101万人，增加693万人。其中，参加职工基本医疗保险人数34423万人，增加1498万人；参加城乡居民基本医疗保险人数101678万人。参加失业保险人数21689万人，增加1147万人。年末全国领取失业保险金人数270万人。参加工伤保险人数26770万人，增加1291万人，其中参加工伤保险的农民工8934万人，增加318万人。参加生育保险人数23546万人，增加2129万人。年末全国共有805万人享受城市最低生活保障，3621万人享受农村最低生活保障，447万人享受农村特困人员[50]救助供养，全年临时救助[51]1341万人次。全年资助8990万人参加基本医疗保险，实施直接救助[52]7300万人次。全年国家抚恤、补助退役军人和其他优抚对象837万人。

年末全国共有各类提供住宿的社会服务机构4.1万个，其中养老机构3.8万个，儿童服务机构735个。社会服务床位[53]850.9万张，其中养老服务床位823.8万张，儿童服务床位9.8万张。年末共有社区服务中心2.9万个，社区服务站39.3万个。

十、科学技术和教育

全年研究与试验发展（R&D）经费支出24426亿元，比上年增长10.3%，与国内生产总值之比为2.40%，其中基础研究经费1504亿元。国家科技重大专项共安排198个项目（课题），国家自然科学基金共资助4.57万个项目。截至年末，正在运行的国家重点实验室522个，国家工程研究中心（国家工程实验室）350个，国家企业技术中心1636家，大众创业万众创新示范基地212家。国家级科技企业孵化器[54]1173家，国家备案众创空间[55]2386家。全年授予专利权363.9万件，比上年增长40.4%；PCT专利申请受理量[56]7.2万件。截至年末，有效专利1219.3万件，其中境内有效发明专利221.3万件，预计每万人口发明专利拥有量15.8件。全年商标注册576.1万件，比上年下降10.1%。全年共签订技术合同55万项，技术合同成交金额28252亿元，比上年增长26.1%。

[50] 农村特困人员是指无劳动能力，无生活来源，无法定赡养、抚养、扶养义务人或者其法定义务人无履行义务能力的农村老年人、残疾人以及未满16周岁的未成年人。

[51] 临时救助是指国家对遭遇突发事件、意外伤害、重大疾病或其他特殊原因导致基本生活陷入困境，其他社会救助制度暂时无法覆盖或救助之后基本生活暂时仍有严重困难的家庭或个人给予的应急性、过渡性的救助。

[52] 包括医保部门实施的住院救助、门诊救助和其他有关部门实施的直接救助。

[53] 社会服务床位数除收养性机构外，还包括救助类机构、社区类机构的床位。

[54] 国家级科技企业孵化器是指符合《科技企业孵化器管理办法》规定的，以促进科技成果转化、培育科技企业和企业家精神为宗旨，提供物理空间、共享设施和专业化服务的科技创业服务机构，且经过科技部批准确定的科技企业孵化器。

[55] 国家备案众创空间是指符合《发展众创空间工作指引》规定的新型创新创业服务平台，且按照《国家众创空间备案暂行规定》经科技部审核备案的众创空间。

[56] PCT专利申请受理量是指国家知识产权局作为PCT专利申请受理局受理的PCT专利申请数量。PCT(Patent Cooperation Treaty)即专利合作条约，是专利领域的一项国际合作条约。

图 18 2016–2020 年研究与试验发展（R&D）经费支出及其增长速度

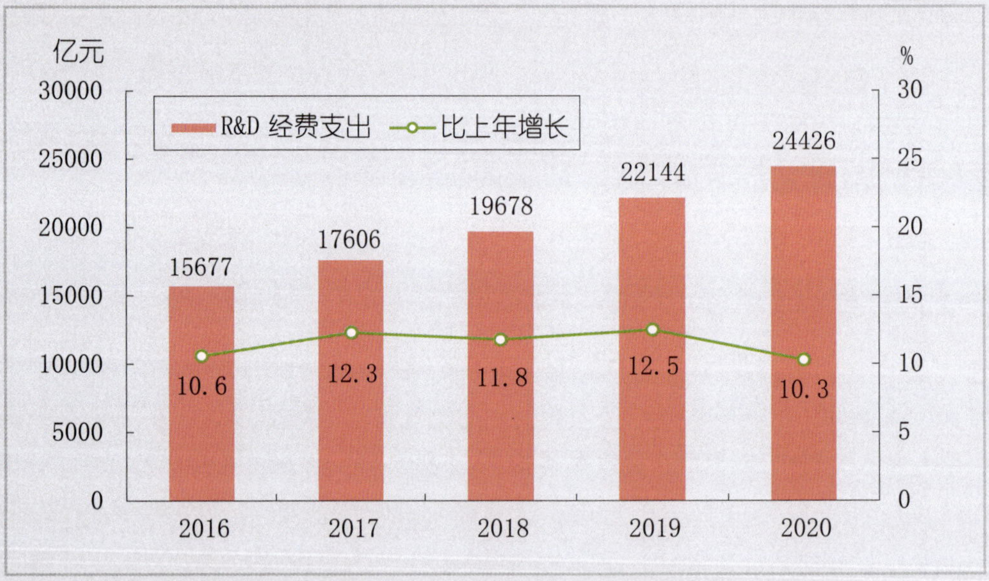

表 15 2020 年专利授权和有效专利情况

指　标	专利数（万件）	比上年增长（%）
专利授权数	**363.9**	**40.4**
其中：境内专利授权	350.4	42.6
其中：发明专利授权	53.0	17.1
其中：境内发明专利	43.4	22.5
年末有效专利数	**1219.3**	**25.4**
其中：境内有效专利	1111.5	27.9
其中：有效发明专利	305.8	14.5
其中：境内有效发明专利	221.3	18.8

全年成功完成35次宇航发射。嫦娥五号发射成功，首次完成我国月表采样返回。我国首次火星探测任务“天问一号”探测器成功发射。500米口径球面射电望远镜（FAST）正式开放运行。北斗三号全球卫星导航系统正式开通。量子计算原型系统“九章”成功研制。全海深载人潜水器“奋斗者”号完成万米深潜。

年末全国共有国家质检中心852家。全国现有产品质量、体系和服务认证机构724个，累计完成对79万家企业的认证。全年制定、修订国家标准2252项，其中新制定1584项。全年制造业产品质量合格率[57]为93.39%。

[57]制造业产品质量合格率是指以产品质量检验为手段，按照规定的方法、程序和标准实施质量抽样检测，判定为质量合格的样品数占全部抽样样品数的百分比，统计调查样本覆盖制造业的29个行业。

全年研究生教育招生 110.7 万人，在学研究生 314.0 万人，毕业生 72.9 万人。普通本专科招生 967.5 万人，在校生 3285.3 万人，毕业生 797.2 万人。中等职业教育[58]招生 644.7 万人，在校生 1663.4 万人，毕业生 484.9 万人。普通高中招生 876.4 万人，在校生 2494.5 万人，毕业生 786.5 万人。初中招生 1632.1 万人，在校生 4914.1 万人，毕业生 1535.3 万人。普通小学招生 1808.1 万人，在校生 10725.4 万人，毕业生 1640.3 万人。特殊教育招生 14.9 万人，在校生 88.1 万人，毕业生 12.1 万人。学前教育在园幼儿 4818.3 万人。九年义务教育巩固率为 95.2%，高中阶段毛入学率为 91.2%。

图 19　2016—2020 年普通本专科、中等职业教育及普通高中招生人数

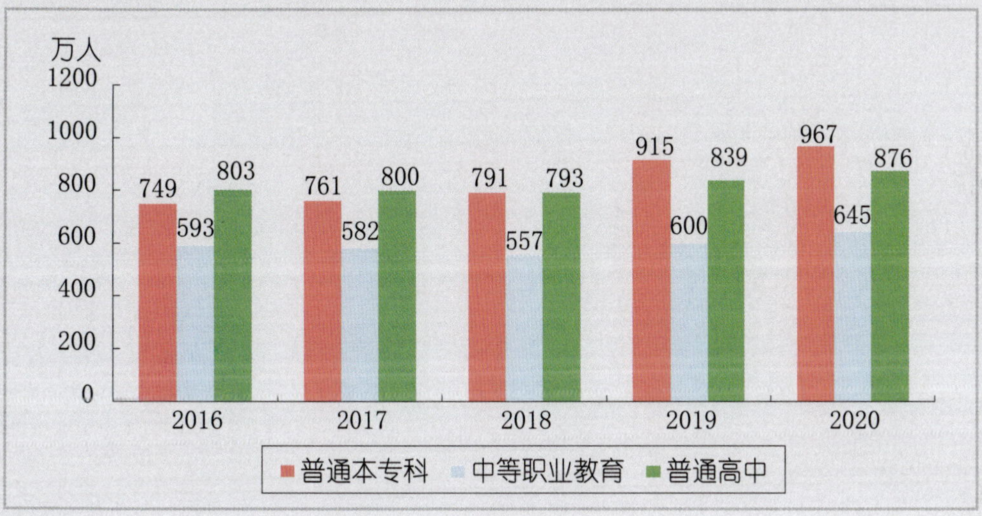

十一、文化旅游、卫生健康和体育

年末全国文化和旅游系统共有艺术表演团体 2027 个，博物馆 3510 个。全国共有公共图书馆 3203 个，总流通[59]56953 万人次；文化馆 3327 个。有线电视实际用户 2.10 亿户，其中有线数字电视实际用户 2.01 亿户。年末广播节目综合人口覆盖率为 99.4%，电视节目综合人口覆盖率为 99.6%。全年生产电视剧 202 部 7476 集，电视动画片 116688 分钟。全年生产故事影片 531 部，科教、纪录、动画和特种影片[60]119 部。出版各类报纸 277 亿份，各类期刊 20 亿册，图书 101 亿册（张），预计人均图书拥有量[61]7.24 册（张）。年末全国共有档案馆 4234 个，已开放各类档案 17659 万卷（件）。全年全国规模以上文化及相关产业企业营业收入 98514 亿元，按可比口径计算，比上年增长 2.2%。

[58] 中等职业教育包括普通中专、成人中专、职业高中和技工学校。

[59] 总流通人次是指本年度内到图书馆场馆接受图书馆服务的总人次，包括借阅书刊、咨询问题以及参加各类读者活动等。

[60] 特种影片是指采用与常规影院放映在技术、设备、节目方面不同的电影展示方式，如巨幕电影、立体电影、立体特效（4D）电影、动感电影、球幕电影等。

[61] 人均图书拥有量是指在一年内全国平均每人能拥有的当年出版图书册数。

全年国内游客28.8亿人次，比上年下降52.1%。其中，城镇居民游客20.7亿人次，下降53.8%；农村居民游客8.1亿人次，下降47.0%。国内旅游收入22286亿元，下降61.1%。其中，城镇居民游客花费17967亿元，下降62.2%；农村居民游客花费4320亿元，下降55.7%。

图20 2016-2020年国内游客人次及其增长速度

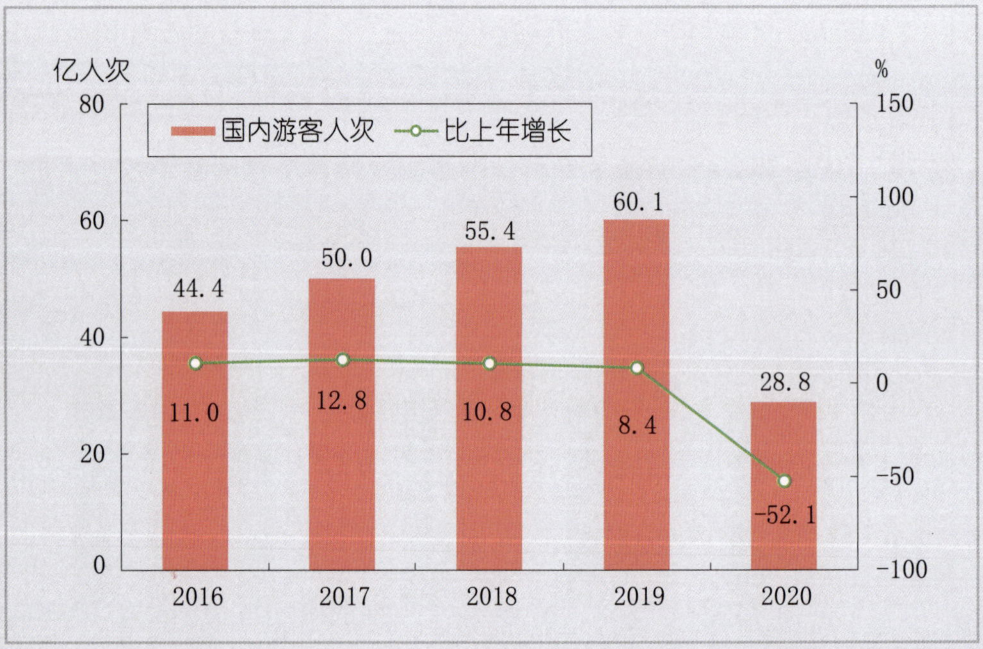

年末全国共有医疗卫生机构102.3万个，其中医院3.5万个，在医院中有公立医院1.2万个，民营医院2.4万个；基层医疗卫生机构97.1万个，其中乡镇卫生院3.6万个，社区卫生服务中心（站）3.5万个，门诊部（所）29.0万个，村卫生室61.0万个；专业公共卫生机构1.4万个，其中疾病预防控制中心3384个，卫生监督所（中心）2736个。年末卫生技术人员1066万人，其中执业医师和执业助理医师408万人，注册护士471万人。医疗卫生机构床位911万张，其中医院713万张，乡镇卫生院139万张。全年总诊疗人次[62]78.2亿人次，出院人数[63]2.3亿人。截至年末，全国累计报告新型冠状病毒肺炎确诊病例87071例，累计治愈出院病例82067例，累计死亡4634人。全国共有8177家医疗卫生机构提供新型冠状病毒核酸检测服务，总检测能力达到1153万份／天。

[62] 总诊疗人次是指所有诊疗工作的总人次数，包括门诊、急诊、出诊、预约诊疗、单项健康检查、健康咨询指导（不含健康讲座）人次。

[63] 出院人数是指报告期内所有住院后出院的人数，包括医嘱离院、医嘱转其他医疗机构、非医嘱离院、死亡及其他人数，不含家庭病床撤床人数。

图 21　2016-2020 年年末卫生技术人员人数

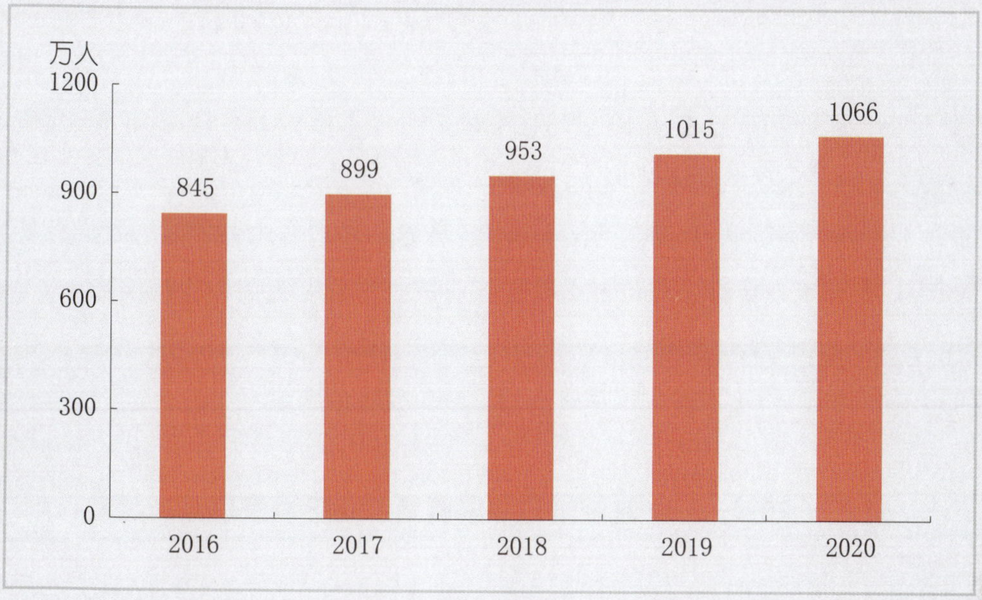

年末全国共有体育场地[64]371.3 万个，体育场地面积[65]31.0 亿平方米，预计人均体育场地面积 2.20 平方米。全年我国运动员在 3 个运动大项中获得 4 个世界冠军，共创 1 项世界纪录[66]。全年我国残疾人运动员在 6 项国际赛事中获得 24 个世界冠军[67]。全年全国 7 岁及以上人口中经常参加体育锻炼人数比例[68]达 37.2%。

十二、资源、环境和应急管理

全年全国国有建设用地供应总量[69]65.8 万公顷，比上年增长 5.5%。其中，工矿仓储用地 16.7 万公顷，增长 13.6%；房地产用地[70]15.5 万公顷，增长 9.3%；基础设施用地 33.7 万公顷，增长 0.3%。

全年水资源总量 30963 亿立方米。

[64] 体育场地调查对象不包括军队、铁路系统所属体育场地。

[65] 体育场地面积是指体育训练、比赛、健身场地的有效面积。

[66] 受新型冠状病毒肺炎疫情影响，2020 年国际级体育赛事大幅减少，我国运动员获世界冠军数和创世界纪录数比往年有所减少。

[67] 2020 年 1—3 月份的国际赛事数据（受新型冠状病毒肺炎疫情影响，2020 年 4 月份以后停止参加国际赛事）。

[68] 经常参加体育锻炼人数比例来源于 2020 年全民健身活动状况调查。经常参加体育锻炼的人是指每周参加体育锻炼频度 3 次及以上，每次体育锻炼持续时间 30 分钟及以上，每次体育锻炼的运动强度达到中等及以上的人。

[69] 国有建设用地供应总量是指报告期内市、县人民政府根据年度土地供应计划依法以出让、划拨、租赁等方式与用地单位或个人签订出让合同或签发划拨决定书、完成交易的国有建设用地总量。

[70] 房地产用地是指商服用地和住宅用地的总和。

全年完成造林面积677万公顷，其中人工造林面积289万公顷，占全部造林面积的42.7%。种草改良面积[71]283万公顷。截至年末，国家级自然保护区474个。新增水土流失治理面积6.0万平方公里。

初步核算，全年能源消费总量49.8亿吨标准煤，比上年增长2.2%。煤炭消费量增长0.6%，原油消费量增长3.3%，天然气消费量增长7.2%，电力消费量增长3.1%。煤炭消费量占能源消费总量的56.8%，比上年下降0.9个百分点；天然气、水电、核电、风电等清洁能源消费量占能源消费总量的24.3%，上升1.0个百分点。重点耗能工业企业单位电石综合能耗下降2.1%，单位合成氨综合能耗上升0.3%，吨钢综合能耗下降0.3%，单位电解铝综合能耗下降1.0%，每千瓦时火力发电标准煤耗下降0.6%。全国万元国内生产总值二氧化碳排放下降1.0%。

图22　2016–2020年清洁能源消费量占能源消费总量的比重

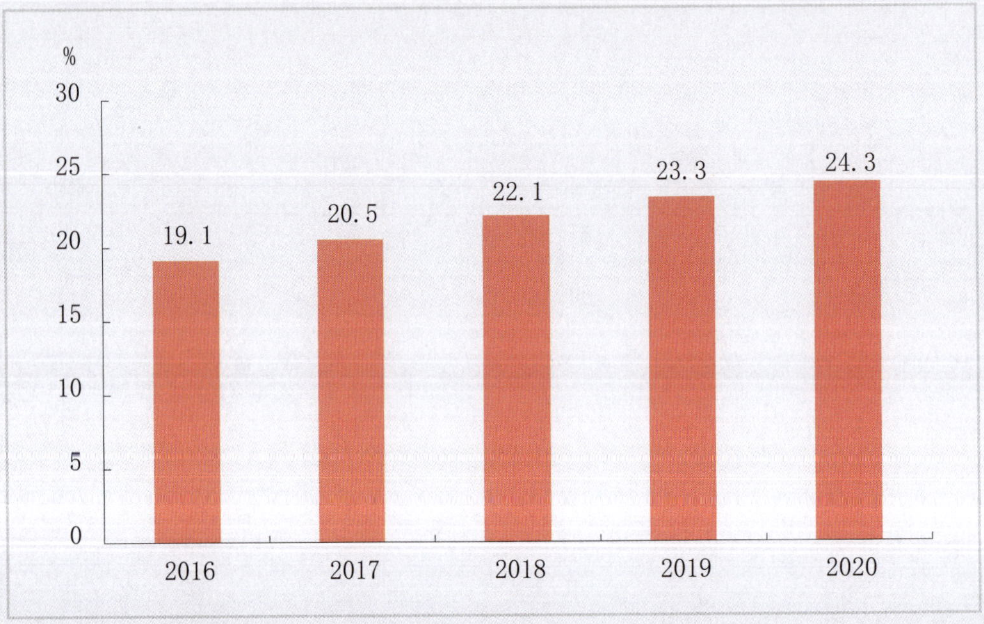

全年近岸海域海水水质[72]达到国家一、二类海水水质标准的面积占77.4%，三类海水占7.7%，四类、劣四类海水占14.9%。

在开展城市区域声环境监测的324个城市中，全年声环境质量好的城市占4.3%，较好的占66.4%，一般的占28.7%，较差的占0.6%。

全年平均气温为10.25℃，比上年下降0.09℃。共有5个台风登陆。

---

[71] 种草改良面积是指通过实施播种、栽种等措施增加牧草数量的面积以及通过压盐压碱压沙、土壤改良、围栏封育等措施使草原原生植被、生态得到改善的面积之和。

[72] 近岸海域海水水质采用面积法进行评价。

全年农作物受灾面积 1996 万公顷，其中绝收 271 万公顷。全年因洪涝和地质灾害造成直接经济损失 2686 亿元，因旱灾造成直接经济损失 249 亿元，因低温冷冻和雪灾造成直接经济损失 154 亿元，因海洋灾害造成直接经济损失 8 亿元。全年大陆地区共发生 5.0 级以上地震 20 次，成灾 5 次，造成直接经济损失约 18 亿元。全年共发生森林火灾 1153 起，受害森林面积约 0.9 万公顷。

全年各类生产安全事故共死亡 27412 人。工矿商贸企业就业人员 10 万人生产安全事故死亡人数 1.301 人，比上年下降 11.7%；煤矿百万吨死亡人数 0.059 人，下降 28.9%。道路交通事故万车死亡人数 1.66 人，下降 7.8%。

资料来源：

本公报中城镇新增就业、城镇登记失业率、社会保障、技工学校数据来自人力资源和社会保障部；外汇储备、汇率数据来自国家外汇管理局；环境监测、万元国内生产总值二氧化碳排放等数据来自生态环境部；财政数据来自财政部；市场主体、质量检验、国家标准制定修订、制造业产品质量合格率数据来自国家市场监督管理总局；水产品产量、新增高效节水灌溉面积数据来自农业农村部；木材产量、造林面积、种草改良面积、国家级自然保护区数据来自国家林业和草原局；新增耕地灌溉面积、水资源总量、新增水土流失治理面积数据来自水利部；发电装机容量、新增220千伏及以上变电设备、电力消费量数据来自中国电力企业联合会；港口货物吞吐量、港口集装箱吞吐量、公路运输、水运、新改建高速公路里程、港口万吨级码头泊位新增通过能力数据来自交通运输部；铁路运输、新建铁路投产里程、增新建铁路复线投产里程、电气化铁路投产里程数据来自中国国家铁路集团有限公司；民航、新增民用运输机场数据来自中国民用航空局；民用汽车、道路交通事故数据来自公安部；邮政业务数据来自国家邮政局；通信业、软件业务收入、新增光缆线路长度等数据来自工业和信息化部；互联网上网人数、互联网普及率数据来自中国互联网络信息中心；棚户区改造、建档立卡贫困户脱贫攻坚农村危房改造数据来自住房和城乡建设部；货物进出口数据来自海关总署；服务进出口、外商直接投资、对外直接投资、对外承包工程、对外劳务合作等数据来自商务部；减税降费数据来自国家税务总局；货币金融、公司信用类债券数据来自中国人民银行；境内交易场所筹资数据来自中国证券监督管理委员会；保险业数据来自中国银行保险监督管理委员会；医疗保险、生育保险、资助参加基本医疗保险、实施直接救助数据来自国家医疗保障局；城乡低保、农村特困人员救助供养、临时救助、社会服务数据来自民政部；优抚对象数据来自退役军人事务部；国家科技重大专项、国家重点实验室、国家级科技企业孵化器、国家备案众创空间、技术合同等数据来自科学技术部；国家自然科学基金资助项目数据来自国家自然科学基金委员会；国家工程研究中心（国家工程实验室）、国家企业技术中心、大众创业万众创新示范基地等数据来自国家发展和改革委员会；专利、商标数据来自国家知识产权局；宇航发射数据来自国家国防科技工业局；教育数据来自教育部；艺术表演团体、博物馆、公共图书馆、文化馆、旅游数据来自文化和旅游部；电视、广播数据来自国家广播电视总局；电影数据来自国家电影局；报纸、期刊、图书数据来自国家新闻出版署；档案数据来自国家档案局；医疗卫生数据来自国家卫生健康委员会；体育数据来自国家体育总局；残疾人运动员数据来自中国残疾人联合会；国有建设用地供应、海洋灾害造成直接经济损失数据来自自然资源部；平均气温、台风登陆数据来自中国气象局；农作物受灾面积、洪涝和地质灾害造成直接经济损失、旱灾造成直接经济损失、低温冷冻和雪灾造成直接经济损失、森林火灾、受害森林面积、生产安全事故数据来自应急管理部；地震次数、地震灾害造成直接经济损失数据来自中国地震局；其他数据均来自国家统计局。

STATISTICAL COMMUNIQUÉ OF THE PEOPLE'S REPUBLIC OF CHINA ON THE 2020 NATIONAL ECONOMIC AND SOCIAL DEVELOPMENT[1]

National Bureau of Statistics of China
February 28, 2021

The year of 2020 was an unusual year in the history of the People's Republic of China, as the country faces complicated international situations, arduous tasks in seeking reform, development and stability at home and heavy blows from the COVID-19 epidemic in particular. The Central Committee of the Communist Party of China (CPC) with Comrade Xi Jinping as the core made the overall planning, maintained strategic focus, made accurate judgement on situations and well-planned deployment, took decisive actions, paid arduous efforts, and made major and timely decisions on coordinating efforts to advance both the epidemic prevention and control and economic and social development. Under the guidance of Xi Jinping Thought on Socialism with Chinese Characteristics for a New Era, all regions and departments fully implemented the spirit of the 19th National Congress of the CPC and the second, third, fourth and fifth plenary sessions

1. All figures in this Communiqué are preliminary statistics. Statistics in this Communiqué do not include Hong Kong SAR, Macao SAR and Taiwan Province. Due to the rounding-off reasons, the subentries may not add up to the aggregate totals.

of the 19th Central Committee of the CPC, followed the decisions and arrangements made by the CPC Central Committee and the State Council, responded to the risks and challenges composedly, committed unswervingly to the high-quality development, and coordinated efforts to advance both the epidemic prevention and control and economic and social development. All regions and departments took solid steps to stabilize employment, financial operation, foreign trade, foreign investment, domestic investment and market expectations (six areas), and fully safeguarded employment, basic living needs, operation of market entities, food and energy security, stable industrial and supply chains and the normal functioning of primary-level governments (six fronts). As a result, the economy recovered to normal quarter by quarter, making China the only major economy with positive economic growth in the world. With a complete victory in the fight of poverty reduction and decisive accomplishments in building a moderately prosperous society in all respects, China has made historic achievements that have satisfied the people and impressed the world.

I. General Outlook[2]

According to preliminary estimation, the gross domestic product (GDP)[3] in 2020 was 101,598.6 billion yuan, up by 2.3 percent over the previous year. Of this total, the value added of the primary industry was 7,775.4 billion yuan, up by 3.0 percent, that of the secondary industry was 38,425.5 billion yuan, up by 2.6 percent and that of the tertiary industry was 55,397.7 billion yuan, up by 2.1 percent. The value added of the primary industry accounted for 7.7 percent of the GDP; that of the secondary industry accounted for 37.8 percent; and that of the tertiary industry accounted for 54.5 percent. The contribution of the final consumption expenditure to GDP growth rate was down by 0.5 percentage points, that of the gross capital formation up by 2.2 percentage points and that of the net exports of goods and services up by 0.7 percentage points. By quarter, GDP in the first quarter was down by 6.8 percent year on year, up by 3.2 percent in the second quarter, up by 4.9 percent in the third quarter, and up by 6.5 percent in the fourth quarter. The per capita GDP in 2020 was expected to be 72,447 yuan, up by 2.0 percent over the previous year. The gross national income[4] in 2020 was 100,915.1 billion yuan, up by 1.9 percent over the previous year. The national energy

2. Statistics of the seventh National Population Census undertaken in 2020 will be released in April 2021. Therefore, data about population and employment were not released in this Communiqué and the per capita data in this Communiqué were based on an estimate of the population.

3. Gross domestic product (GDP), value added of the three and related industries, regional GDP, per capita GDP and gross national income (GNI) as quoted in this Communiqué are calculated at current prices whereas their growth rates are at constant prices.

4. Gross national income, also known as gross national product, refers to the total primary distribution of the income created by all the resident units of a country (or a region) during a certain period of time. It equals to gross domestic product plus the net primary distribution of income from abroad.

consumption per 10,000 yuan worth of GDP[5] went down by 0.1 percent over 2019, and the overall labor productivity[6] was expected to reach 117,746 yuan per person in 2020, up by 2.5 percent over the previous year.

Figure 1: Gross Domestic Product and Growth Rates 2016-2020

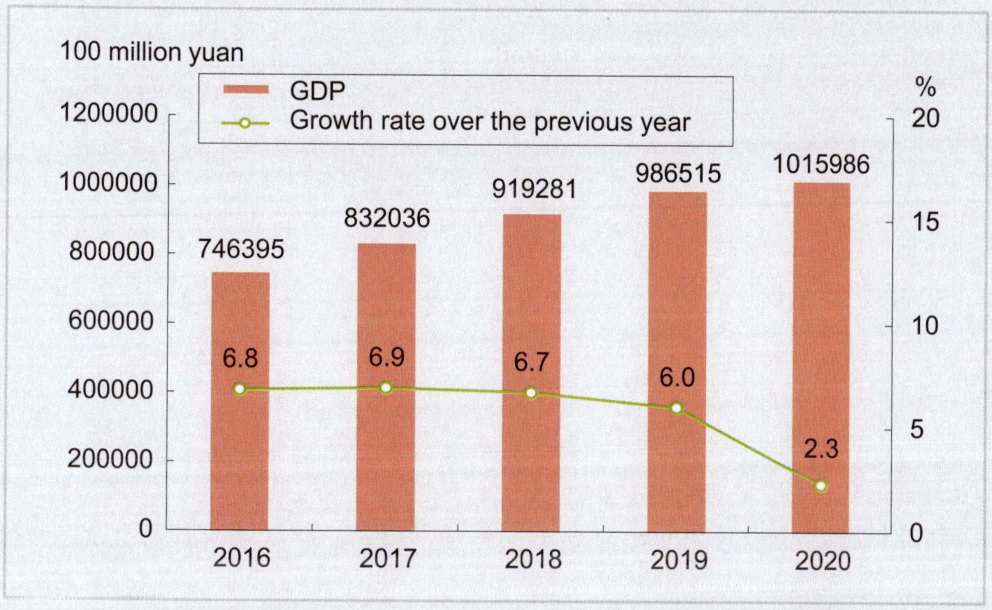

Figure 2: Shares of the Three Industries' Value Added of GDP 2016-2020

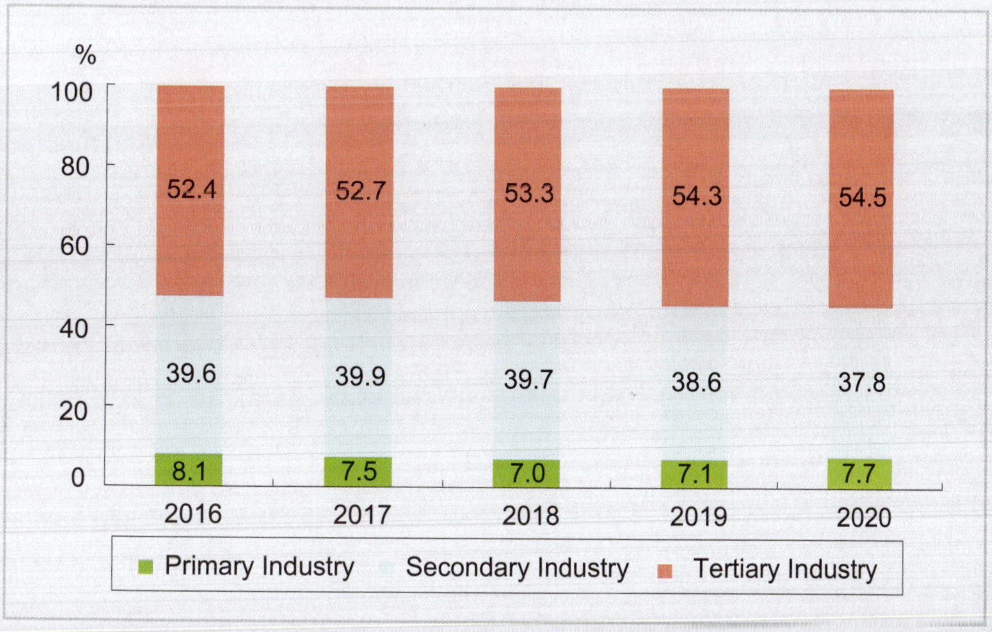

5. The national energy consumption per 10,000 yuan worth of GDP is calculated at constant prices of 2015.

6. The overall labor productivity refers to the ratio between the GDP (at 2015 constant prices) and the total number of persons employed. The number of persons employed in 2020 was an estimate.

The newly increased employed people in urban areas numbered 11.86 million, 1.66 million less than the previous year. The surveyed urban unemployment rate was 5.2 percent at the year end, and the registered urban unemployment rate was 4.2 percent. The total number of migrant workers[7] was 285.60 million, down by 1.8 percent over that of 2019. Specifically, the number of migrant workers who left their hometowns and worked in other places was 169.59 million, down by 2.7 percent, and those who worked in their own localities reached 116.01 million, down by 0.4 percent.

Figure 3: Newly Increased Employed People in Urban Areas 2016-2020

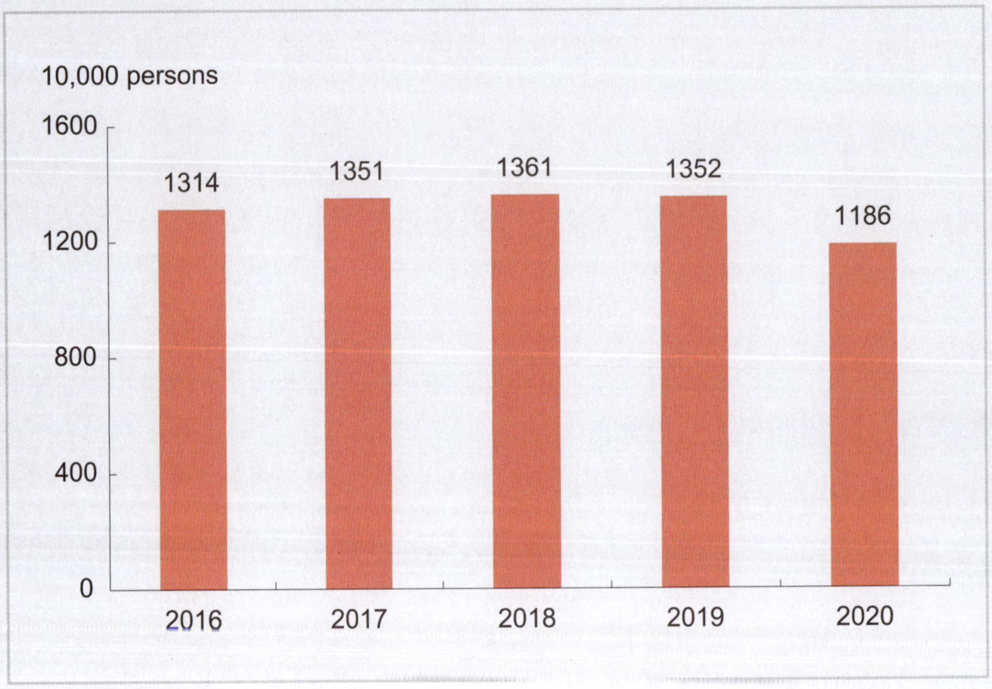

The consumer prices in 2020 went up by 2.5 percent over the previous year. The producer prices for industrial products went down by 1.8 percent and the purchasing prices for industrial producers down by 2.3 percent. The producer prices for farm products[8] increased by 15.0 percent. In December, out of the 70 large and medium-sized cities, 60 cities experienced a year-on-year rise in sales prices of new commercial residential buildings and 10 cities experienced a decline.

7. The number of migrant workers includes those who are employed outside their villages and towns for more than six months in the year and those who are engaged in non-agricultural work in their villages and towns for more than six months in the year.

8. The producer prices for farm products refer to the prices of farm products sold directly by producers.

Figure 4: Monthly Changes of Consumer Prices in 2020

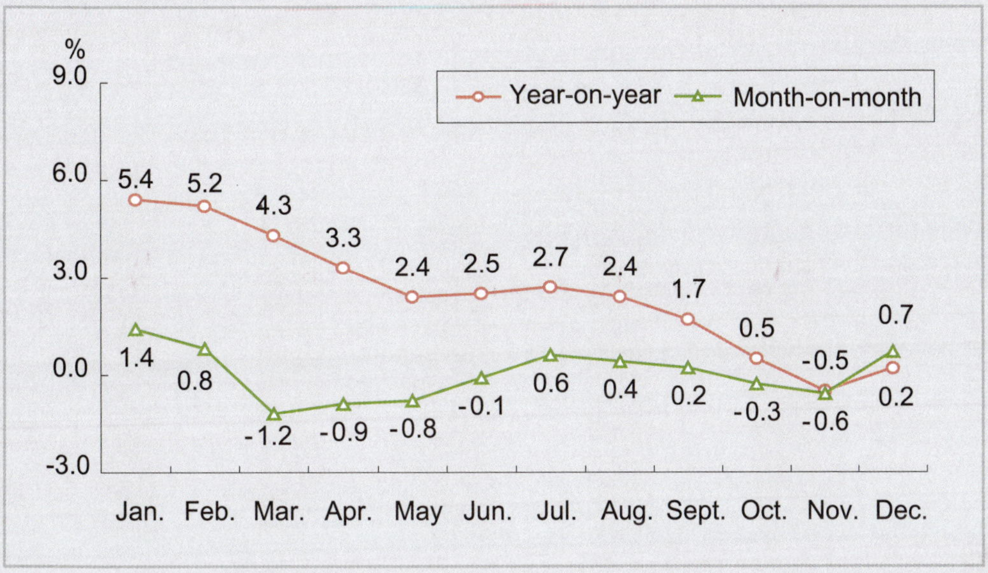

Table 1: Changes of Consumer Prices in 2020

Unit: %

Item	National Average	Urban	Rural
General level of consumer prices	**2.5**	**2.3**	**3.0**
Of which: Food, tobacco and liquor	8.3	7.8	9.6
Clothing	-0.2	-0.2	-0.3
Residence[9]	-0.4	-0.4	-0.5
Household facilities, articles and services	0.0	0.1	-0.1
Transportation and telecommunication	-3.5	-3.6	-3.2
Education, culture and recreation	1.3	1.4	1.1
Health care and medical services	1.8	1.7	2.0
Miscellaneous goods and services	4.3	4.4	4.1

At the end of 2020, China's foreign exchange reserves reached 3,216.5 billion US dollars, an increase of 108.6 billion US dollars compared with that at the end of 2019. The average exchange rate of the year was 6.8974 RMB to 1 USD dollar, appreciated by 0.02 percent over that of 2019.

9. The prices for residence include prices for rent, maintenance and management, water, electricity and fuel etc.

Figure 5: Year-end China's Foreign Exchange Reserves 2016-2020

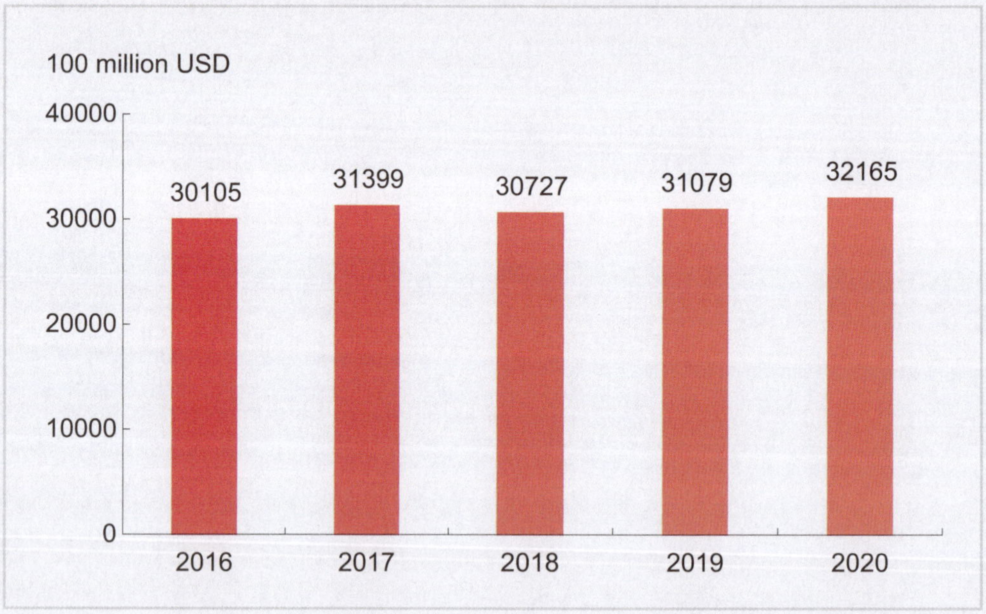

Decisive achievements were made in the three critical battles. Based on the current rural poverty line of an individual's cost of living per year of 2,300 yuan (at 2010 constant prices), 5.51 million rural population living in poverty were lifted out of poverty. Since the 18th National Congress of the Communist Party of China, the absolute poverty was eradicated historically with 98.99 million rural poor population and all poverty-stricken counties lifted out of poverty. In 2020, the per capita disposable income of rural residents in impoverished areas[10] was 12,588 yuan, up by 8.8 percent over the previous year, or a real growth of 5.6 percent after deducting price factors. Of the monitored 337 cities at prefecture level and above, 59.9 percent reached the air quality standard and 40.1 percent failed. The annual average concentration of particulate matter ($PM_{2.5}$) for cities that failed to meet the standard (based on the 262 cities that failed to meet the standard of annual average $PM_{2.5}$ concentration in 2015) was 37 micrograms per cubic meter, down by 7.5 percent over that of the previous year. In 2020, of the 1,940 sections under the national monitoring program for surface water, 83.4 percent were fairly clean water quality (Grade I to III), 13.6 percent were Grade IV, 2.4 percent were Grade V and 0.6 percent was worse than Grade V national standard. By the end of 2020, the outstanding liability of local governments nationwide was within the limit approved by the National People's Congress. Major progress have been made in financial risks management.

10. Impoverished areas cover contiguous poverty-stricken areas and key counties under national poverty alleviation and development program beyond those areas. There were 832 counties altogether. Since 2017, Aksu Prefecture in Xinjiang has also been covered in poverty monitoring.

New industries, new types of business and new business models grew despite headwinds. Among the industries above the designated size, the value added of high technology manufacturing industry[11] grew by 7.1 percent over the previous year, accounting for 15.1 percent of that of all industrial enterprises above the designated size. The value added for the manufacture of equipment[12] was up by 6.6 percent, accounting for 33.7 percent of that of all industrial enterprises above the designated size. Among the service enterprises above the designated size[13], the business revenue of the strategic emerging service industries[14] went up by 8.3 percent over the previous year. In 2020, the investment in high technology industries[15] increased by 10.6 percent over the previous year. The output of new energy vehicles in 2020 reached 1.456 million, up by 17.3 percent over the previous year, and that of integrated circuits was 261.47 billion, up by 29.6 percent. In 2020, the online retail sales[16] reached 11,760.1 billion yuan, an increase of 10.9 percent over the previous year on a comparable basis. In 2020, the number of newly registered market entities was 25.02 million with 22 thousand market entities newly registered per day on average. By the end of 2020, the market entities totaled 140 million.

Regional coordinated development was pushed forward steadily. By the end of 2020, the urbanization rate of permanent residents exceeded 60 percent. By region[17], in 2020, the gross domestic product in the

11. High technology manufacturing industry includes manufacture of medicine, manufacture of aerospace vehicle and equipment, manufacture of electronic and communication equipment, manufacture of computers and office equipment, manufacture of medical equipment, manufacture of measuring instrument and equipment and manufacture of optical and photographic equipment.

12. Manufacture of equipment includes manufacture of metal products, general purpose equipment, special purpose equipment, automobiles, railway, ship, aerospace and other transport equipment, electrical machinery and apparatus, computers, communication and other electric equipment and measuring instrument and machinery.

13. Service enterprises above the designated size, refer to legal entities of transport, storage and post, information transmission, software and information technology services, water conservancy, environment and public facilities management, and health with annual business revenue of 20 million yuan or above; legal entities of real estate (excluding real estate development and operation), leasing and business services, scientific research and technology services and education with annual business revenue of 10 million yuan or above; and legal entities of services to households, repair and other services and culture, sports and entertainment, and social work with annual business revenue of 5 million yuan or above.

14. Strategic emerging service industries refer to the related service sectors of information technology of new generation, manufacture of high-end equipment, new materials, biotech, new energy vehicles, new energy, energy-saving and environmental protection and digital creative industries, and service industries related to new technology and new entrepreneurship. The growth rate of the business revenue of the strategic emerging service industries in 2020 is calculated on a comparable basis.

15. Investment in high technology industries refers to investment in six high technology manufacturing industries, including the manufacture of medicine and manufacture of aerospace vehicle and equipment, and nine high technology service industries, including information service and e-commerce service.

16. Online retail sales refer to the retail sales of goods and services realized through internet trading platforms (online platforms mainly in trading physical commodities, including self-built websites and third-party platforms).

17. The eastern areas include 10 provinces and municipalities: Beijing, Tianjin, Hebei, Shanghai, Jiangsu, Zhejiang, Fujian, Shandong, Guangdong and Hainan; the central areas cover 6 provinces: Shanxi, Anhui, Jiangxi, Henan, Hubei and Hunan; the western areas include 12 provinces, autonomous regions and municipalities: Inner Mongolia, Guangxi, Chongqing, Sichuan, Guizhou, Yunnan, Tibet, Shaanxi, Gansu, Qinghai, Ningxia and Xinjiang; the northeastern areas include 3 provinces: Liaoning, Jilin and Heilongjiang.

eastern areas was 52,575.2 billion yuan, an increase of 2.9 percent compared with the previous year; the central areas, 22,224.6 billion yuan, up by 1.3 percent; the western areas, 21,329.2 billion yuan, up by 3.3 percent; and the northeastern areas, 5,112.5 billion yuan, up by 1.1 percent. In 2020, the gross domestic product in Beijing-Tianjin-Hebei Region reached 8,639.3 billion yuan, up by 2.4 percent over the previous year; that in the Yangtze River Economic Belt, 47,158.0 billion yuan, up by 2.7 percent; and that in the Yangtze River Delta, 24,471.4 billion yuan, up by 3.3 percent. Major regional strategies like construction of Guangdong-Hong Kong-Macao Greater Bay Areas, ecological protection in Yellow River Basin and high-quality development were further implemented.

II. Agriculture

In 2020, the sown area of grain was 116.77 million hectares, an increase of 0.70 million hectares compared with that in 2019. Of this total, the sown area of rice was 30.08 million hectares, an increase of 0.38 million hectares; the sown area of wheat was 23.38 million hectares, a decrease of 0.35 million hectares; the sown area of corn was 41.26 million hectares, a decrease of 20 thousand hectares. The sown area of cotton was 3.17 million hectares, a decrease of 0.17 million hectares. The sown area of oil-bearing crops was 13.13 million hectares, up by 0.20 million hectares; the sown area of sugar crops was 1.57 million hectares, down by 40 thousand hectares.

The total output of grain in 2020 was 669.49 million tons, an increase of 5.65 million tons over the previous year, or up by 0.9 percent. Of this total, the output of summer crops was 142.86 million tons, up by 0.9 percent, and that of the early rice was 27.29 million tons, up by 3.9 percent. The output of autumn grain was 499.34 million tons, up by 0.7 percent. The output of cereal in 2020 was 616.74 million tons, up by 0.5 percent over 2019, among which the output of rice was 211.86 million tons, up by 1.1 percent; that of wheat was 134.25 million tons, up by 0.5 percent; and that of corn was 260.67 million tons, roughly the same but a little less than that of 2019.

Figure 6: Output of Grain 2016-2020

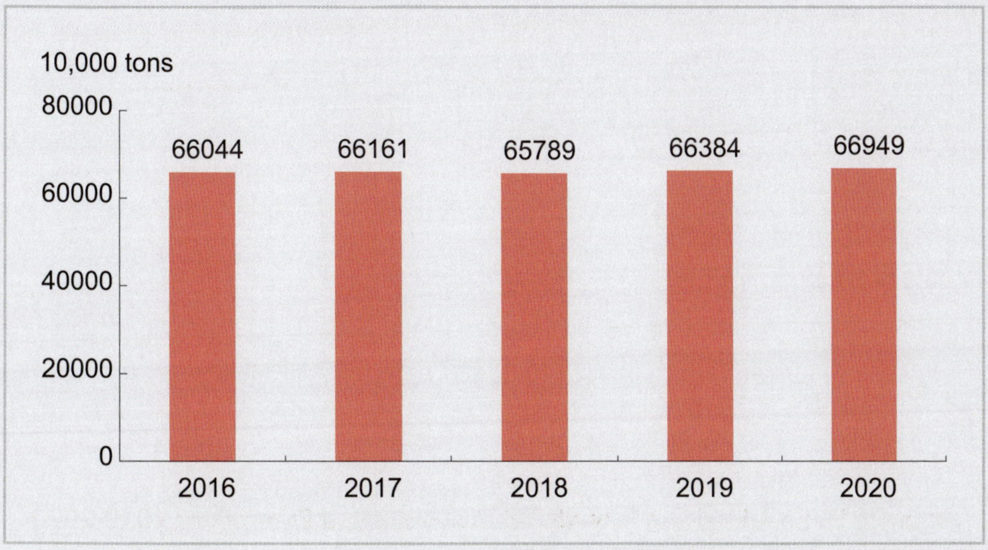

In 2020, the output of cotton was 5.91 million tons, up by 0.4 percent over the previous year, that of oil-bearing crops was 35.85 million tons, up by 2.6 percent, that of sugar crops was 120.28 million tons, down by 1.2 percent, and that of tea was 2.97 million tons, up by 7.1 percent.

The total output of pork, beef, mutton and poultry in 2020 was 76.39 million tons, down by 0.1 percent over the previous year. Of this total, the output of pork was 41.13 million tons, down by 3.3 percent; that of beef was 6.72 million tons, up by 0.8 percent; that of mutton was 4.92 million tons, up by 1.0 percent; and that of poultry was 23.61 million tons, up by 5.5 percent. The total output of eggs was 34.68 million tons, up by 4.8 percent. The production of milk was 34.40 million tons, up by 7.5 percent. At the end of the year, 406.50 million pigs were registered in the total stocks, up by 31.0 percent compared with that at the end of 2019, and 527.04 million pigs were slaughtered, down by 3.2 percent over the previous year.

The total output of aquatic products in 2020 was 65.45 million tons, up by 1.0 percent over the previous year. Of this total, the output of cultured aquatic products was 52.15 million tons, up by 3.0 percent; and that of fished aquatic products was 13.30 million tons, down by 5.0 percent.

The total production of timber in 2020 reached 87.27 million cubic meters, down by 13.1 percent over the previous year.

In 2020, over 0.43 million hectares of farmland were newly equipped with irrigation systems and another 1.60 million hectares of farmland was newly equipped with water-saving irrigation systems.

III. Industry and Construction

In 2020, the total value added of the industrial sector was 31,307.1 billion yuan, up by 2.4 percent over the previous year. The value added of industrial enterprises above the designated size increased by 2.8 percent. Of the industrial enterprises above the designated size, in terms of ownership, the value added of the state-holding enterprises grew by 2.2 percent, that of the share-holding enterprises up by 3.0 percent, that of the enterprises funded by foreign investors and investors from Hong Kong, Macao and Taiwan up by 2.4 percent and that of private enterprises up by 3.7 percent. In terms of sectors, the value added of the mining industry was up by 0.5 percent, that of manufacturing up by 3.4 percent and that of production and supply of electricity, heat power, gas and water up by 2.0 percent.

Figure 7: Value Added and Growth Rates of Industrial Enterprises 2016-2020

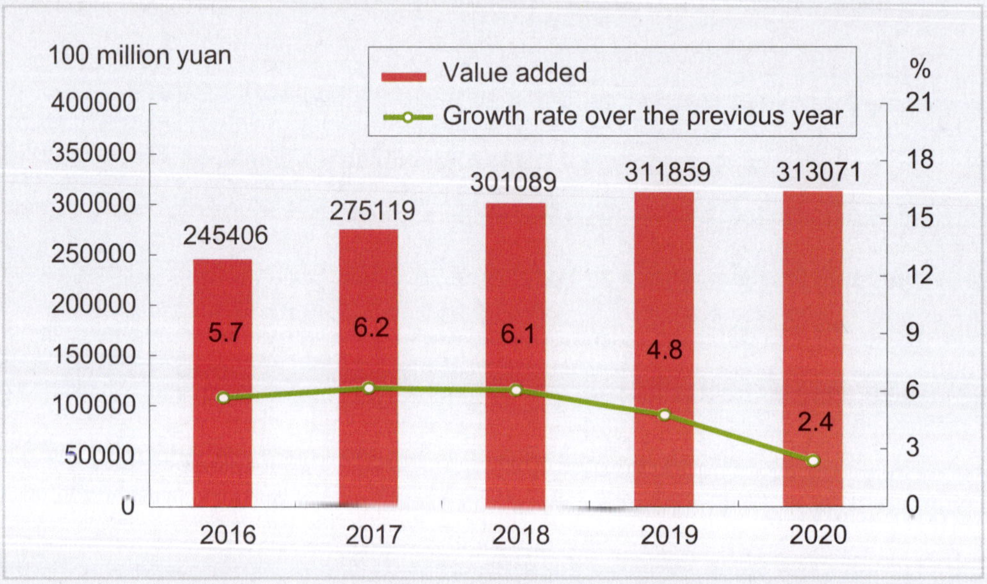

In 2020, of the industrial enterprises above the designated size, the value added for processing of food from agricultural and sideline products was down by 1.5 percent over the previous year; for textile industry up by 0.7 percent; for manufacture of raw chemical materials and chemical products up by 3.4 percent; for manufacture of non-metallic mineral products up by 2.8 percent; for smelting and pressing of ferrous metals up by 6.7 percent; for manufacture of general purpose machinery up by 5.1 percent; for manufacture of special purpose machinery up by 6.3 percent; for manufacture of automobiles up by 6.6 percent; for manufacture of electrical machinery and apparatus up by 8.9 percent; for manufacture of computers, communication equipment and other electronic equipment up by 7.7 percent; for production and supply of electricity and heat power up by 1.9 percent.

Table 2: Output of Major Industrial Products and Growth Rates in 2020[18]

Product	Unit	Output	Increase over 2019 (%)
Yarn	10000 tons	2618.3	-7.4
Cloth	100 million meters	460.3	-17.1
Chemical fiber	10000 tons	6126.5	4.1
Refined sugar (final product)	10000 tons	1431.3	3.0
Cigarettes	100 million	23863.7	0.9
Color TV sets	10000	19626.2	3.3
Of which: LCD TV sets	10000	19247.2	3.0
Household refrigerators	10000	9014.7	14.0
Air conditioners	10000	21035.3	-3.8
Primary energy output	100 million tons of standard coal equivalent	40.8	2.8
Coal	100 million tons	39.0	1.4
Crude petroleum oil	10000 tons	19476.9	1.6
Natural gas	100 million cubic meters	1925.0	9.8
Electricity	100 million kilowatt-hours	77790.6	3.7
Of which: Thermal power[19]	100 million kilowatt-hours	53302.5	2.1
Hydropower	100 million kilowatt-hours	13552.1	3.9
Nuclear-power	100 million kilowatt-hours	3662.5	5.1
Crude steel	10000 tons	106476.7	7.0
Rolled steel[20]	10000 tons	132489.2	10.0
Ten kinds of nonferrous metals	10000 tons	6188.4	5.5
Of which: Refined copper (copper)	10000 tons	1002.5	2.5
Aluminum electrolyze	10000 tons	3708.0	5.6
Cement	100 million tons	24.0	2.5
Sulfuric acid (100%)	10000 tons	9238.2	1.3
Caustic soda (100%)	10000 tons	3673.9	6.2
Ethylene	10000 tons	2160.0	5.2
Chemical fertilizers (100 percent equivalent)	10000 tons	5496.0	-4.1
Power generation equipment	10000 kilowatts	13226.2	38.3
Motor vehicles	10000	2532.5	-1.4
Of which: Basic passenger cars (cars)	10000	923.9	-10.2
Sport utility vehicles (SUVs)	10000	905.0	2.6
Large and medium tractors	10000	34.6	23.0
Integrated circuits	100 million pieces	2614.7	29.6
Program-controlled switchboards	10000 lines	702.5	-11.1
Mobile telephones	10000	146961.8	-13.3
Micro computer equipment	10000	37800.4	10.6
Industrial robots	10000 sets	21.2	20.7

18. Output data of some products were verified and adjusted in 2019; the growth rates of output in 2020 are calculated on a comparable basis.

19. Thermal power refers to electricity generated by coal, oil, gas, residual heat, pressure and gas, waste incineration and biomass.

20. The data include 305.66 million tons of steel which has been reprocessed among enterprises.

By the end of 2020, the installed power generation capacity was 2,200.58 million kilowatts, up by 9.5 percent over that at the end of 2019, among which[21] the installed thermal power generation capacity was 1,245.17 million kilowatts, up by 4.7 percent; the installed hydropower generation capacity was 370.16 million kilowatts, up by 3.4 percent; the installed nuclear power generation capacity was 49.89 million kilowatts, up by 2.4 percent. The installed grid-connected wind power generation capacity was 281.53 million kilowatts, up by 34.6 percent and the installed grid-connected solar power generation capacity was 253.43 million kilowatts, up by 24.1 percent.

In 2020, the profits made by industrial enterprises above the designated size were 6,451.6 billion yuan, up by 4.1 percent[22] over the previous year. By ownership, the profits of state-holding enterprises were 1,486.1 billion yuan, down by 2.9 percent over the previous year; those of share-holding enterprises were 4,544.5 billion yuan, up by 3.4 percent; those of enterprises funded by foreign investors or investors from Hong Kong, Macao and Taiwan were 1,823.4 billion yuan, up by 7.0 percent; and those of private enterprises were 2,026.2 billion yuan, up by 3.1 percent. In terms of different sectors, the profits of mining were 355.3 billion yuan, down by 31.5 percent over the previous year; those of manufacturing were 5,579.5 billion yuan, up by 7.6 percent; and those of the production and supply of electricity, heat power, gas and water were 516.8 billion yuan, up by 4.9 percent. In 2020, the cost for per-hundred-yuan business revenue of the industrial enterprises above the designated size was 83.89 yuan, or 0.11 yuan less than that of 2019; the profit rate of the business revenue was 6.08 percent, up by 0.20 percentage points. By the end of 2020, the asset-liability ratio of industrial enterprises above the designated size was 56.1 percent, 0.3 percentage points lower than the end of 2019. The national industrial capacity utilization rate[23] was 74.5 percent in 2020, specifically 67.3 percent, 74.4 percent, 76.7 percent and 78.0 percent in the first, second, third and fourth quarters.

In 2020, the value added of construction enterprises in China was 7,299.6 billion yuan, up by 3.5 percent over the previous year. The profits made by construction enterprises qualified for general contracts and specialized contracts reached 830.3 billion yuan, up by 0.3 percent over the previous year, of which the profits made by state-holding enterprises were 287.1 billion yuan, up by 4.7 percent.

---

21. Some installed power generation capacity was not listed (e.g. geothermal).

22. The growth rates and rate changes of financial indicators of industrial enterprises above the designated size in 2020 are calculated on a comparable basis due to adjustments of data coverage in the statistical programmes, statistical law enforcement and removal of duplicated data.

23. Capacity utilization rate refers to the ratio of the actual production to the production capacity (in terms of value). Actual production refers to the total industrial output value during the enterprise's reporting period. Production capacity refers to the production which can be realized and sustained for a long term under the condition of the supply of labor force, materials, fuel and transportation guaranteed and the production equipment in proper operation.

Figure 8: Value Added and Growth Rates of Construction Industry 2016-2020

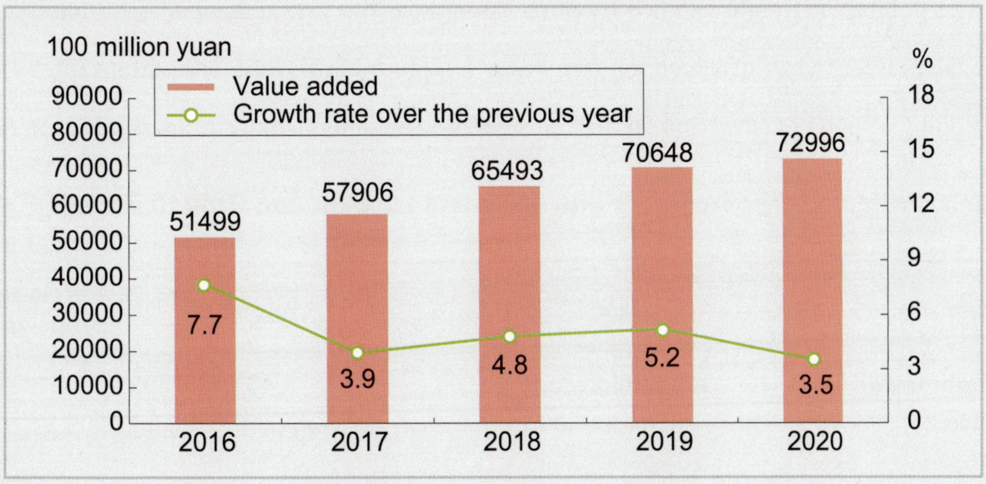

IV. Service Sector

In 2020, the value added of the wholesale and retail trades was 9,568.6 billion yuan, down by 1.3 percent over the previous year; that of transport, storage and post was 4,156.2 billion yuan, up by 0.5 percent; that of hotels and catering services was 1,597.1 billion yuan, down by 13.1 percent; that of financial intermediation was 8,407.0 billion yuan, up by 7.0 percent; that of real estate was 7,455.3 billion yuan, up by 2.9 percent; that of information transmission, software and information technology services was 3,795.1 billion yuan, up by 16.9 percent; and that of leasing and business services was 3,161.6 billion yuan, down by 5.3 percent. In 2020, the business revenue of service enterprises above the designated size grew by 1.9 percent over the previous year, and the operating profits decreased by 7.0 percent.

Figure 9: Value Added and Growth Rates of Service Sector 2016-2020

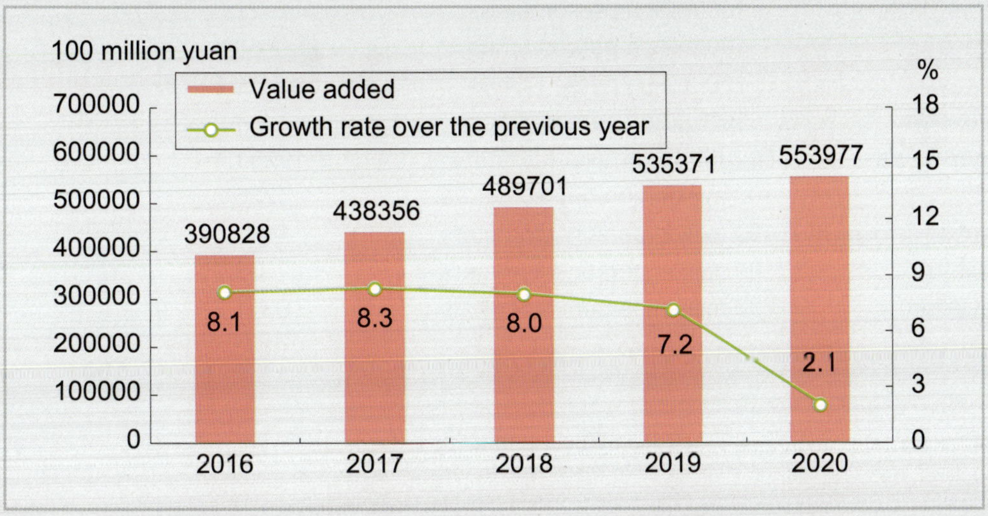

The total freight traffic[24] in 2020 reached 46.3 billion tons. The freight flows were 19,661.8 billion ton-kilometers. The volume of freight handled by ports throughout the year totaled 14.5 billion tons, up by 4.3 percent over the previous year, of which the freight for foreign trade was 4.5 billion tons, up by 4.0 percent. Container shipping of ports reached 264.30 million standard containers, up by 1.2 percent.

Table 3: Freight Traffic by All Means of Transportation and Growth Rates in 2020

Item	Unit	Volume	Increase over 2019(%)
Total freight traffic	**100 million tons**	**463.4**	**-0.5**
Railways	100 million tons	44.6	3.2
Highways	100 million tons	342.6	-0.3
Waterways	100 million tons	76.2	-3.3
Civil aviation	10000 tons	676.6	-10.2
Freight flows	**100 million ton-kilometers**	**196618.3**	**-1.0**
Railways	100 million ton-kilometers	30371.8	1.0
Highways	100 million ton-kilometers	60171.8	0.9
Waterways	100 million ton-kilometers	105834.4	-2.5
Civil aviation	100 million ton-kilometers	240.2	-8.7

In 2020, the total passenger traffic was 9.7 billion person-times, down by 45.1 percent over 2019, and the passenger flows were 1,925.1 billion person-kilometers, down by 45.5 percent.

Table 4: Passenger Traffic by All Means of Transportation and Growth Rates in 2020

Item	Unit	Volume	Increase over 2019(%)
Total passenger traffic	**100 million person-times**	**96.7**	**-45.1**
Railways	100 million person-times	22.0	-39.8
Highways	100 million person-times	68.9	-47.0
Waterways	100 million person-times	1.5	-45.2
Civil aviation	100 million person-times	4.2	-36.7
Passenger flows	**100 million person-kilometers**	**19251.4**	**-45.5**
Railways	100 million person-kilometers	8266.2	-43.8
Highways	100 million person-kilometers	4641.0	-47.6
Waterways	100 million person-kilometers	33.0	-58.0
Civil aviation	100 million person-kilometers	6311.2	-46.1

24. The total freight traffic and flows include the traffic and flows by railways, highways, waterways and civil aviation and the growth rates in 2020 are calculated on a comparable basis. Due to the change of data source of certain pipeline transportation of petroleum and gas caused by the foundation of PipeChina, data of pipeline transportation are being verified.

The total number of motor vehicles for civilian use reached 280.87 million (including 7.48 million tri-wheel motor vehicles and low-speed trucks) by the end of 2020, up by 19.37 million over that at the end of 2019, of which the privately-owned vehicles numbered 243.93 million, an increase of 17.58 million. The total number of cars for civilian use was 156.40 million, an increase of 9.96 million, of which the privately-owned cars numbered 146.74 million, an increase of 9.73 million.

The turnover of post services[25] totaled 2,105.3 billion yuan, up by 29.7 percent over the previous year. In 2020, the number of mail delivery was 1.42 billion; that of parcel delivery was 20 million; and that of express delivery was 83.36 billion with a revenue reaching 879.5 billion yuan. The turnover of telecommunication services[26] totaled 13,675.8 billion yuan, up by 28.1 percent over the previous year. By the end of 2020, there were 1,775.98 million phone subscribers in China, of whom 1,594.07 million were mobile phone subscribers. Mobile phone coverage was 113.9 sets per 100 persons. The number of fixed broadband internet users[27] reached 483.55 million, an increase of 34.27 million over the end of the previous year. Of this total, fixed fiber-optic broadband internet users[28] amounted to 454.14 million, an increase of 36.75 million. The mobile internet traffic in 2020 was 165.6 billion gigabytes, up by 35.7 percent over the previous year. The number of internet user was 989 million at the end of 2020, 986 million of which were mobile internet surfers[29]. The coverage of internet was 70.4 percent, and 55.9 percent in rural areas. Software revenue from software and information technology services industry[30] in 2020 was 8,161.6 billion yuan, up by 13.3 percent over 2019 on a comparable basis.

25. The turnover of post services is calculated at constant prices of 2010.

26. The turnover of telecommunication services is calculated at constant prices of 2015.

27. Fixed broadband internet users refer to those who subscribed to the telecommunication enterprises and access the Internet through xDSL, FTTx+LAN, FTTH/0 and other broadband access ways as well as general dedicated lines at the end of the reporting period.

28. Fixed fiber-optic broadband internet users refer to those who subscribed to the telecommunication enterprises and access the Internet through FTTH or FTT0 at the end of the reporting period.

29. The number of mobile internet surfers refers the number of people who have accessed the internet through mobile phones.

30. Software and information technology services industry includes software development, integrated circuit design, information system integration and internet of things technology services, operation maintenance services, information processing and storage support services, IT consulting services, digital content services and other IT services industry.

Figure 10: Express Delivery and Growth Rates 2016-2020

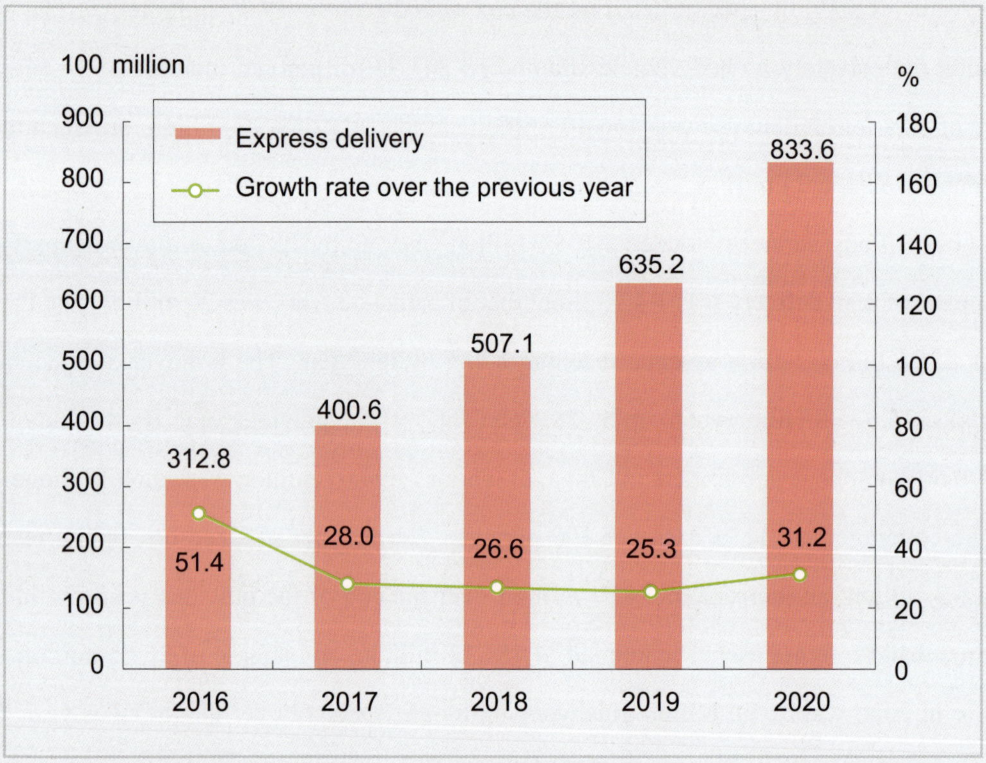

Figure 11: Year-end Number of Fixed Broadband Internet Users 2016-2020

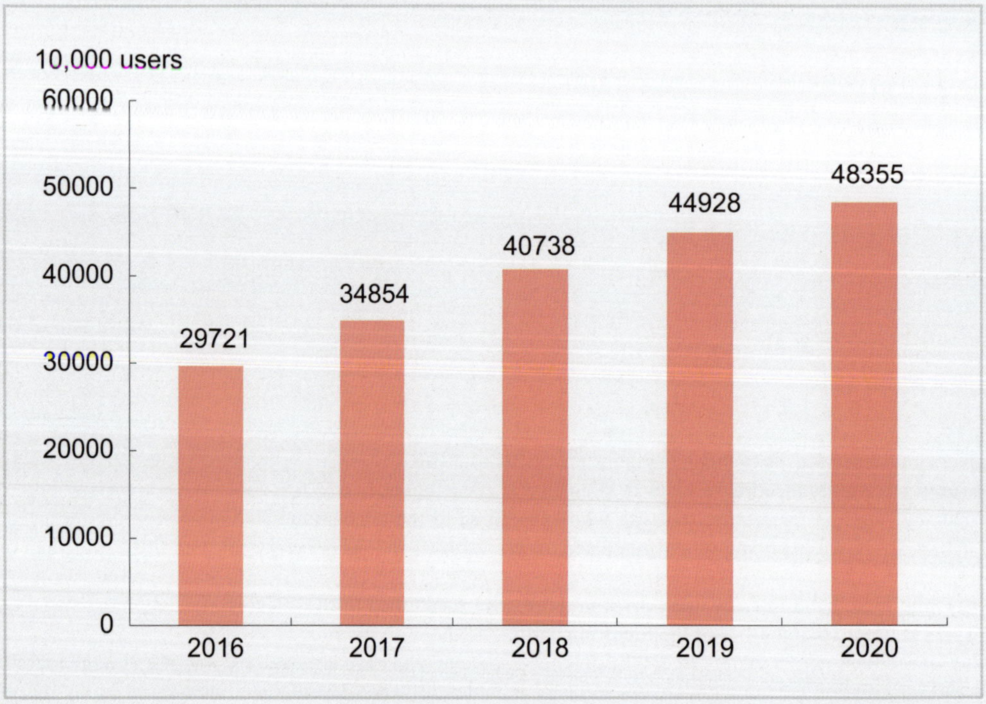

V. Domestic Trade

In 2020, the total retail sales of consumer goods reached 39,198.1 billion yuan, a decrease of 3.9 percent over the previous year. An analysis on different areas showed that the retail sales of consumer goods in urban areas stood at 33,911.9 billion yuan, down by 4.0 percent, and that in rural areas reached 5,286.2 billion yuan, down by 3.2 percent. Grouped by consumption patterns, the retail sales of commodities was 35,245.3 billion yuan, down by 2.3 percent, and that of catering industry was 3,952.7 billion yuan, down by 16.6 percent.

Figure 12: Total Retail Sales of Consumer Goods 2016-2020[31]

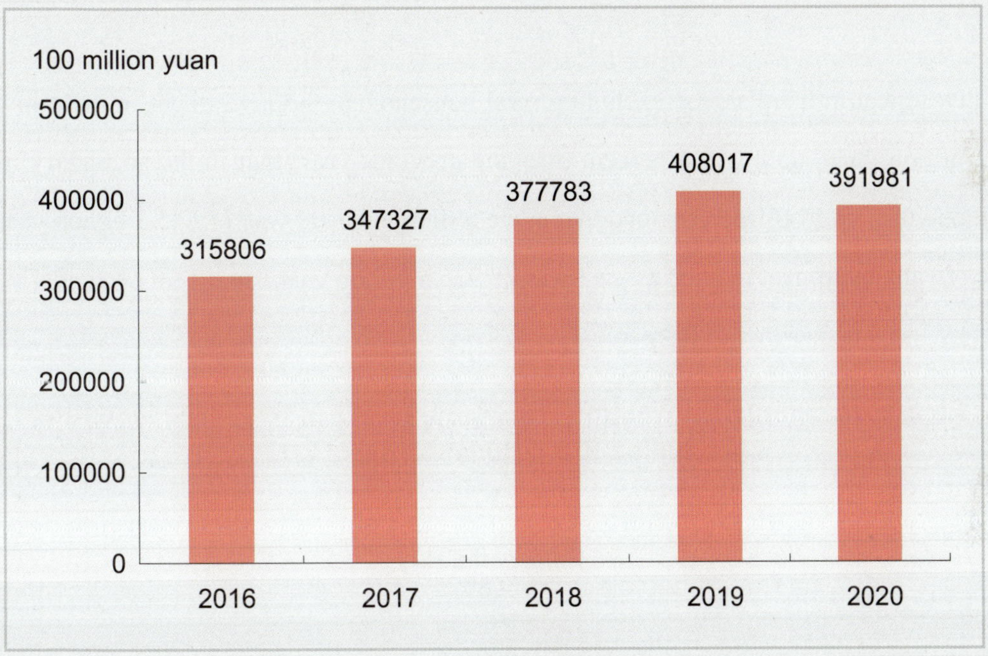

Of the total retail sales of commodities by enterprises above the designated size, the year-on-year growth of retail sales for grain, oil and food went up by 9.9 percent; beverage up by 14.0 percent; tobacco and liquor up by 5.4 percent; clothes, shoes, hats and textiles down by 6.6 percent; cosmetics up by 9.5 percent; gold, silver and jewelry down by 4.7 percent; daily necessities up by 7.5 percent; household appliances and audio-video equipment down by 3.8 percent; traditional Chinese and western medicines up by 7.8 percent; cultural and office appliances up by 5.8 percent; furniture down by 7.0 percent; telecommunication equipment up by 12.9 percent; building and decoration materials down by 2.8 percent; petroleum and petroleum products down by 14.5 percent; and motor vehicles down by 1.8 percent.

31. The total retail sales of consumer goods from 2016 to 2019 have been revised based on the fourth National Economic Census and the related programmes.

In 2020, the online retail sales of physical goods were 9,759.0 billion yuan, up by 14.8 percent over the previous year on a comparable basis, accounting for 24.9 percent of the total retail sales of consumer goods, or 4.0 percentage points higher than that of 2019.

VI. Investment in Fixed Assets

The total investment in fixed assets[32] of the country in 2020 was 52,727.0 billion yuan, up by 2.7 percent over the previous year. Of the total, the investment in fixed assets (excluding rural households) was 51,890.7 billion yuan, up by 2.9 percent. By regions[33], the investment in eastern areas was up by 3.8 percent over the previous year, central areas up by 0.7 percent, western areas up by 4.4 percent, and northeastern areas up by 4.3 percent.

In the investment in fixed assets (excluding rural households), the investment in the primary industry was 1,330.2 billion yuan, up by 19.5 percent over the previous year; that in the secondary industry was 14,915.4 billion yuan, up by 0.1 percent; and that in the tertiary industry was 35,645.1 billion yuan, up by 3.6 percent. The private investment in fixed assets[34] was 28,926.4 billion yuan, up by 1.0 percent. The investment in infrastructure[35] saw an increase of 0.9 percent.

Figure 13: Shares of Investment in Fixed Assets of the Three Industries (Excluding Rural Households) in 2020

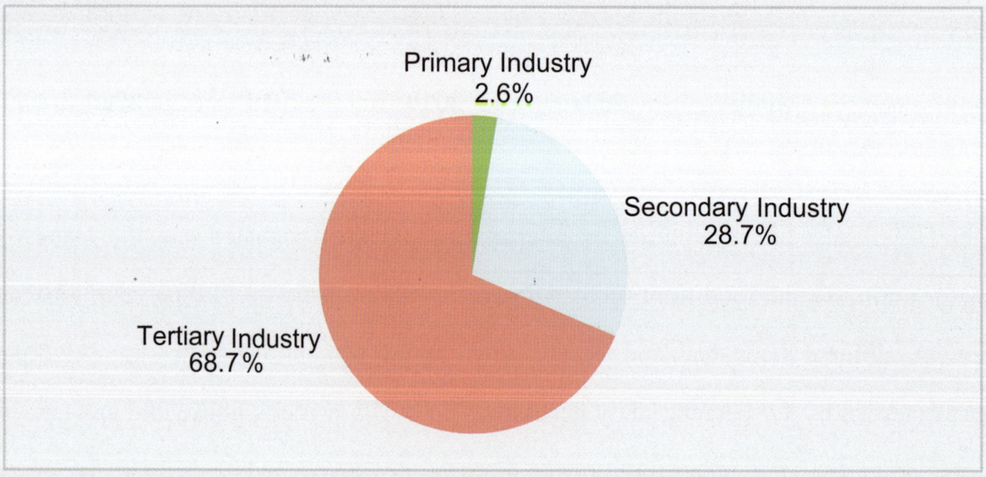

32. The figure of the investment in fixed assets in 2019 was revised according to the results of the fourth National Economic Census, statistical law enforcement and the statistical survey method reform and programmes. The growth rates in 2020 are calculated on a comparable basis.

33. See Note 17.

34. Private investment in fixed assets refers to investment in the construction or purchase of fixed assets by domestic collective, private and individual-owned enterprises and organizations or their holding enterprises (with absolute holding and relative holding enterprises).

35. Investment in infrastructure includes transportation, postal service, telecommunication, radio, TV and satellite transmission, internet and related services, water conservancy, environment and public facilities management.

Table 5: Growth Rates of Investment in Fixed Assets (Excluding Rural Households) by Sectors in 2020

Sector	Increase over 2019 (%)	Sector	Increase over 2019 (%)
Total	**2.9**	Financial Intermediation	-13.3
Agriculture,Forestry, Animal Husbandry and Fishery	19.1	Real Estate[36]	5.0
Mining	-14.1	Leasing and Business Services	5.0
Manufacturing	-2.2	Scientific Research and Technical Services	3.4
Production and Supply of Electricity, Heat Power, Gas and Water	17.6	Water Conservancy, Environment and Public Facilities Management	0.2
Construction	9.2	Services to Households, Repair and Other Services	-2.9
Wholesale and Retail Trades	-21.5	Education	12.3
Transport, Storage and Post	1.4	Health and Social Service	26.8
Hotels and Catering Services	-5.5	Culture, Sports and Entertainment	1.0
Information Transmission, Software and Information Technology Services	18.7	Public Management, Social Security and Social Organizations	-6.4

Table 6: Newly Increased Production and Operation Capacity through Fixed Assets Investment in 2020

Item	Unit	Volume
Newly increased power transformer equipment with a capacity of over 220 kilovolts	10,000 kilovolt-amperes	22288
New railways put into operation	kilometer	4933
Of which: high-speed railways	kilometer	2521
Extended or new double-track railways put into operation	kilometer	3380
Electrified railways put into operation	kilometer	5480
Length of new and rebuilt highways	kilometer	12713
New throughput capacity of berths for over 10,000-tonnage ships	10,000 tons/year	30562
New civil transportation airports	-	3
New lines of optical-fiber cables	10,000 km	428

36. The investment in real estate includes the investment in real estate development, construction of buildings for own use, property management, intermediary services and other real estate investment.

In 2020, the investment in real estate development was 14,144.3 billion yuan, up by 7.0 percent over the previous year. Of this total, the investment in residential buildings reached 10,444.6 billion yuan, an increase of 7.6 percent, that in office buildings was 649.4 billion yuan, up by 5.4 percent, and that in buildings for commercial business was 1,307.6 billion yuan, down by 1.1 percent. The floor space of the commercial buildings for sale was 498.50 million square meters at the end of 2020, an increase of 0.29 million square meters over that at the end of 2019. The floor space of the commercial residential buildings for sale was 223.79 million square meters, a decrease of 0.94 million square meters.

In 2020, 2.09 million housing units were started to be rebuilt in rundown urban areas nationwide. The number of housing units rebuilt in rundown areas was 2.03 million. In rural areas of China, for the poverty-stricken households that had their economic status registered at the local governments, 742.1 thousand[37] of them witnessed their dilapidated houses rebuilt or renovated in 2020 as the round-off of the programme in the fight against poverty.

Table 7: Main Indicators for Real Estate Development and Sales and Growth Rates in 2020

Item	Unit	Volume	Increase over 2019 (%)
Value of Investment	100 million RMB	141443	7.0
Of which: residential buildings	100 million RMB	104446	7.6
Floor space of buildings under construction	10000 square meters	926759	3.7
Of which: residential buildings	10000 square meters	655558	4.4
Floor space of buildings newly started	10000 square meters	224433	-1.2
Of which: residential buildings	10000 square meters	164329	-1.9
Floor space of buildings completed	10000 square meters	91218	-4.9
Of which: residential buildings	10000 square meters	65910	-3.1
Floor space of commercial buildings sold	10000 square meters	176086	2.6
Of which: residential buildings	10000 square meters	154878	3.2
Funds for investment this year	100 million RMB	193115	8.1
Of which: domestic loans	100 million RMB	26676	5.7
individual mortgage	100 million RMB	29976	9.9

37. The number of housing units of the poverty-stricken rural households with their economic status registered at the local governments that were started to be rebuilt or renovated includes the 641.6 thousand units in stock from 2019 and another 100.5 thousand unit found in the re-examination of the poverty reduction.

VII. Foreign Economic Relations

The total value of imports and exports of goods in 2020 reached 32,155.7 billion yuan, up by 1.9 percent over that of the previous year. Of this total, the value of goods exported was 17,932.6 billion yuan, up by 4.0 percent; the value of goods imported was 14,223.1 billion yuan, down by 0.7 percent. The surplus of trade in goods reached 3,709.6 billion yuan, up by 797.6 billion yuan over that of the previous year. The total value of imports and exports between China and countries along the Belt and Road[38] was 9,369.6 billion yuan, an increase of 1.0 percent over that of the previous year. Of the total, the value of goods exported was 5,426.3 billion yuan, an increase of 3.2 percent; that of goods imported was 3,943.3 billion yuan, a decrease of 1.8 percent.

Figure 14: Imports and Exports of Goods 2016-2020

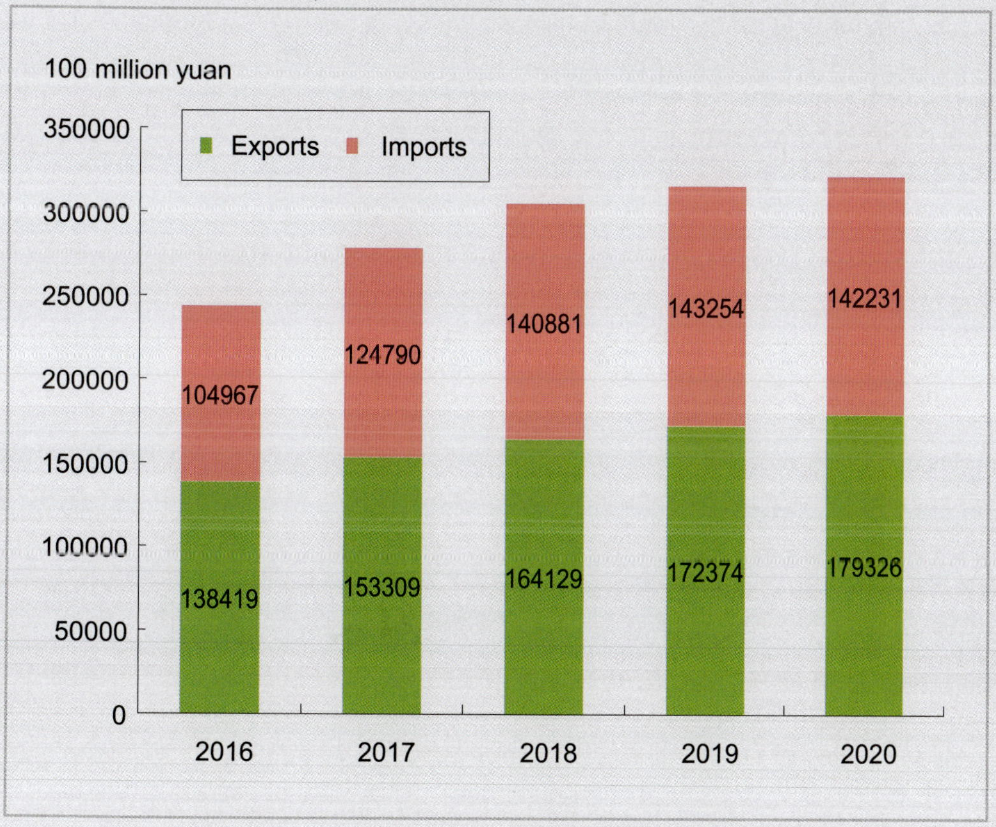

38. The Belt and Road refers to the Silk Road Economic Belt and the 21st Century Maritime Silk Road.

Table 8: Total Value and Growth Rates of Import and Export of Goods in 2020

Item	Value (100 million yuan)	Increase over 2019 (%)
Total value of import and export of goods	**321557**	**1.9**
Exports	179326	4.0
Of which: General trade	106460	6.9
Processing trade	48589	-4.2
Of which: Mechanical and electronic products	106608	6.0
High & new technology products	53692	6.5
Imports	142231	-0.7
Of which: General trade	86048	-0.7
Processing trade	27853	-3.2
Of which: Mechanical and electronic products	65625	4.8
High & new technology products	47160	7.2
Trade surplus	**37096**	—

Table 9: Main Export Commodities in Volume and Value and the Growth Rates in 2020

Item	Unit	Volume	Increase over 2019 (%)	Value (100 million yuan)	Increase over 2019(%)
Rolled steel	10000 tons	5367	-16.5	3151	-14.8
Textile yarns and textile articles	—	—	—	10695	30.4
Clothes and clothing accessories	—	—	—	9520	-6.0
Footwear	10000 pairs	740137	-22.4	2454	-20.9
Furniture and parts	—	—	—	4039	12.2
Luggage and similar containers	10000 tons	201	-34.7	1429	-23.9
Toys	—	—	—	2317	7.7
Plastic articles	—	—	—	5902	20.0
Integrated circuits	100 million pieces	2598	18.8	8056	15.0
Automatic data processing machines and components	—	—	—	14599	12.0
Mobile phones	10000 sets	96640	-2.8	8647	0.4
Containers	10000 units	198	-17.9	508	10.5
Liquid crystal display panels	10000 units	126747	-15.9	1370	-7.1
Motor vehicles (including chassis)	10000 sets	108	-13.2	1090	-3.2

Table 10: Main Import Commodities in Volume and Value and the Growth Rates in 2020

Item	Unit	Volume	Increase over 2019 (%)	Value (100 million yuan)	Increase over 2019 (%)
Soybean	10000 tons	10033	13.3	2743	12.5
Edible vegetable oil	10000 tons	983	3.1	515	17.7
Iron ore and concentrate	10000 tons	117010	9.5	8229	17.8
Coal and lignite	10000 tons	30399	1.5	1411	-12.1
Crude oil	10000 tons	54239	7.3	12218	-26.8
Petroleum products refined	10000 tons	2835	-7.2	818	-30.4
Natural gas	10000 tons	10166	5.3	2315	-19.4
Plastics in primary forms	10000 tons	4063	10.1	3628	-1.2
Paper pulp	10000 tons	3063	12.7	1088	-7.6
Rolled steel	10000 tons	2023	64.4	1165	19.8
Unwrought copper and its alloys	10000 tons	668	34.1	2988	33.4
Integrated circuits	100 million pieces	5435	22.1	24207	14.8
Motor vehicles (including chassis)	10000 sets	93	-11.4	3242	-3.5

Table 11: Imports and Exports of Goods by Major Countries and Regions, the Growth Rates and Proportions in 2020

Country or region	Exports (100 million yuan)	Increase over 2019 (%)	Proportion of the total (%)	Imports (100 million yuan)	Increase over 2019 (%)	Proportion of the total (%)
ASEAN	26550	7.0	14.8	20807	6.9	14.6
European Union[39]	27084	7.2	15.1	17874	2.6	12.6
United States	31279	8.4	17.4	9319	10.1	6.6
Japan	9883	0.1	5.5	12090	2.1	8.5
Republic of Korea	7787	1.8	4.3	11957	0.0	8.4
Hong Kong, China	18830	-2.2	10.5	482	-22.9	0.3
Taiwan, China	4163	9.5	2.3	13873	16.2	9.8
Brazil	2417	-1.5	1.3	5834	5.8	4.1
Russia	3506	2.1	2.0	3960	-6.1	2.8
India	4613	-10.5	2.6	1445	16.7	1.0
South Africa	1055	-7.5	0.6	1422	-20.4	1.0

39. The value of imports and exports of goods by European Union excludes data of the Great Britain, and the growth rate is calculated on a comparable basis.

The total value of imports and exports of services in 2020 was 4,564.3 billion yuan, down by 15.7 percent over that of the previous year. The export value of services was 1,935.7 billion yuan, down by 1.1 percent. The import value of services was 2,628.6 billion yuan, down by 24.0 percent. The trade deficit in imports and exports of services was 692.9 billion yuan.

The year 2020 witnessed the establishment of 38,570 enterprises (excluding banking, securities and insurance) with foreign direct investment, down by 5.7 percent over that of the previous year, and the foreign direct investment actually utilized totaled 1,000.0 billion yuan, up by 6.2 percent, or 144.4 billion US dollars, up by 4.5 percent. Specifically, there were 4,294 newly established enterprises receiving direct investment from countries along the Belt and Road (including the investment in China via some free ports), down by 23.2 percent; and foreign capital directly invested in China reached 57.4 billion yuan, down by 0.3 percent, or 8.3 billion US dollars, down by 1.8 percent. In 2020, the foreign investment actually utilized by high technology industry reached 296.3 billion yuan, up by 11.4 percent, or 42.8 billion US dollars, up by 9.5 percent.

Table 12: Total Value of Foreign Direct Investment (Excluding Banking, Securities and Insurance) and the Growth Rates in 2020

Sector	Enterprises	Increase over 2019 (%)	Actually Utilized Value (100 million yuan)	Increase over 2019 (%)
Total	**38570**	**-5.7**	**10000**	**6.2**
Of which: Agriculture, Forestry, Animal Husbandry and Fishery	493	-0.4	40	4.9
Manufacturing	3732	-30.8	2156	-10.8
Production and Supply of Electricity, Heat Power, Gas and Water	260	-11.9	217	-9.4
Transport, Storage and Post	592	0.2	347	12.1
Information Transmission, Software and Information Technology Services	3521	-18.0	1133	13.3
Wholesale and Retail	10812	-21.9	819	33.3
Real Estate	1190	13.3	1407	-12.5
Leasing and Business Services	7513	30.1	1838	22.6
Services to Households, Repair and Other Services	447	23.8	21	-42.4

In 2020, the non-financial outbound direct investment reached 759.8 billion yuan, down by 0.4 percent over that of the previous year, or 110.2 billion US dollars, down by 0.4 percent. Of this total, that to countries along the Belt and Road reached 17.8 billion US dollars, up by 18.3 percent.

Table 13: Total Value and Growth Rates of Non-financial Outbound Direct Investment in 2020

Sector	Value (100 million US dollars)	Increase over 2019 (%)
Total	**1101.5**	**-0.4**
Of which:Agriculture, Forestry, Animal Husbandry and Fishery	13.9	-9.7
Mining	50.9	-32.3
Manufacturing	199.7	-0.5
Production and Supply of Electricity, Heat Power, Gas and Water	27.8	10.3
Construction	51.6	-39.4
Wholesale and Retail	160.7	27.8
Transport, Storage and Post	26.5	-52.3
Information Transmission, Software and Information Technology Services	67.1	9.6
Real Estate	27.3	-43.4
Leasing and Business Services	417.9	17.5

In 2020, the accomplished business revenue through contracted overseas engineering projects was 1,075.6 billion yuan, down by 9.8 percent over that of the previous year, or 155.9 billion US dollars, down by 9.8 percent. Specifically, the accomplished business revenue from countries along the Belt and Road was 91.1 billion US dollars, a decrease of 7.0 percent, accounting for 58.4 percent of the accomplished business revenue through contracted overseas engineering projects. The number of labor forces sent abroad through overseas labor contracts was 300 thousand.

VIII. Finance and Financial Intermediation

The national general public budget revenue reached 18,289.5 billion yuan in 2020, down by 3.9 percent over that of the previous year, of which tax revenue amounted to 15,431.0 billion yuan, down by 2.3 percent. The national general public budget expenditure reached 24,558.8 billion yuan, up by 2.8 percent over that of the previous year. The year 2020 witnessed a further tax and fee cuts of over 2.5 trillion yuan.

Figure 15: General Public Budget Revenue 2016-2020

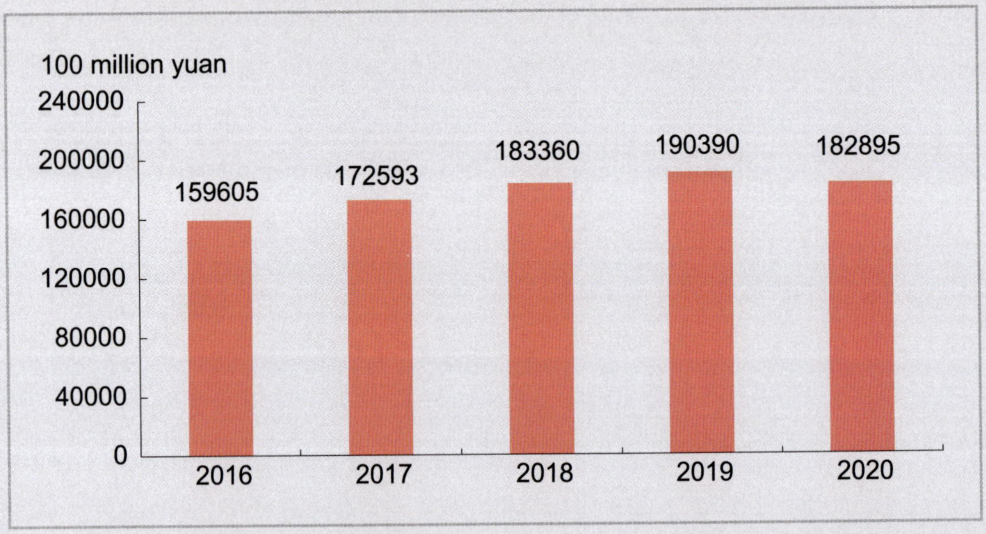

Note: Data for general public budget revenue from 2016 to 2019 as shown in the figure were final accounts and that of 2020 was the executive accounts.

By the end of 2020, money supply of broad sense (M_2) was 218.7 trillion yuan, an increase of 10.1 percent over that by the end of the previous year. Money supply of narrow sense (M_1) was 62.6 trillion yuan, up by 8.6 percent. Cash in circulation (M_0) was 8.4 trillion yuan, up by 9.2 percent.

In 2020, the aggregate financing to the real economy (AFRE) (flow)[40] reached 34.9 trillion yuan, or 9.2 trillion yuan more than that in 2019 on a comparable basis. The AFRE (stock)[41] totaled 284.8 trillion yuan at the end of 2020, up by 13.3 percent over that at the end of 2019 on a comparable basis. Specifically, loans granted to the real economy in Renminbi stood at 171.6 trillion yuan, up by 13.2 percent. Savings deposit in Renminbi and foreign currencies in all items of financial institutions totaled 218.4 trillion yuan at the end of 2020, an increase of 20.2 trillion yuan compared with that at the beginning of the year. Of this total, the savings deposit in Renminbi stood at 212.6 trillion yuan, an increase of 19.6 trillion yuan. Loans in Renminbi and foreign currencies in all items of financial institutions reached 178.4 trillion yuan, an increase of 19.8 trillion yuan. Of this total, loans in Renminbi were 172.7 trillion yuan, an increase of 19.6 trillion yuan. Inclusive finance loans in Renminbi[42] reached 21.5 trillion yuan, an increase of 4.2 trillion yuan.

---

40. The AFRE (flow) refers to the total volume of financing provided by the financial system to the real economy within a certain period of time.

41. The AFRE (stock) refers to the outstanding financing provided by the financial system to the real economy (domestic non-financial enterprises and persons) at the end of a period of time (a month, a quarter or a year).

42. Inclusive finance loans include loans to micro and small businesses with single-client credit line under 10 million yuan, operating loans to self-employed businesses and owners of micro and small businesses, producing and operating loans to farmers, consumption loans to registered people living in poverty, venture guarantee loans and student loans.

Table 14: Savings Deposit and Loans in RMB and Foreign Currencies in All Financial Institutions and Growth Rates at the End of 2020

Item	Year-end figure (100 million yuan)	Increase over 2019 (%)
Savings deposit	**2183744**	**10.2**
Domestic households	934383	13.8
Deposits in RMB	925986	13.9
Domestic non-financial enterprises	688218	10.8
Loans	**1784034**	**12.5**
Domestic short-term loans	492682	4.3
Domestic medium- and long-term loans	1137504	17.1

Loans in Renminbi from rural financial institutions (rural credit cooperatives, rural cooperation banks and rural commercial banks) totaled 21,588.6 billion yuan by the end of 2020, an increase of 2,521.0 billion yuan as compared with that at the beginning of the year. Loans in Renminbi for consumption use from all financial institutions totaled 49,566.8 billion yuan, an increase of 5,599.4 billion yuan. Of the total, short-term personal loans totaled 8,777.4 billion yuan, an increase of 717.7 billion yuan, and medium- and long-term personal loans reached 40,789.4 billion yuan, an increase of 4,881.7 billion yuan.

Funds raised through A-shares issued on Shanghai and Shenzhen Stock Exchanges[43] amounted to 1,541.7 billion yuan in 2020, an increase of 188.3 billion yuan from the previous year. 394 A-shares were newly issued, raising 474.2 billion yuan worth of capital altogether, up by 225.2 billion yuan over that of the previous year. Of the total, 145 shares were from the science and technology innovation board, raising 222.6 billion yuan; refinancing of A-shares (including public newly issued, targeted placement, right issued, preferred stock and exchanged convertible bonds) raised 1,067.4 billion yuan, a decrease of 37.0 billion yuan over that of the previous year. Various types of market entities financed 8,477.7 billion yuan through issuing bonds (including corporate bonds, convertible bonds, exchangeable bonds, financial bonds issued by policy banks, local government bonds and asset-backed securities) on Shanghai and Shenzhen Stock Exchanges, up by 1,279.1 billion yuan over that of the previous year. There were 8,187 companies listed on National

43. Funds raised through Shanghai and Shenzhen Stock Exchanges are calculated by the money raised on the listing date, and the funds raised include the actual exchanged convertible bonds, which were 99.5 billion yuan in 2019 and 119.5 billion yuan in 2020.

Equities Exchange and Quotations[44] and funds raised by listed companies reached 33.9 billion yuan in 2020.

In 2020, 14.2 trillion yuan corporate debenture bonds[45] were issued, an increase of 3.5 trillion yuan over that of the previous year.

The premium of primary insurance received by the insurance companies[46] totaled 4,525.7 billion yuan in 2020, up by 6.1 percent over that of the previous year. Of this total, life insurance premium of primary insurance amounted to 2,398.2 billion yuan, health and casualty insurance premium of primary insurance 934.7 billion yuan, and property insurance premium of primary insurance 1,192.9 billion yuan. Insurance companies paid an indemnity worth of 1,390.7 billion yuan, of which, life insurance indemnity was 371.5 billion yuan, health and casualty insurance indemnity 323.7 billion yuan, and property insurance indemnity 695.5 billion yuan.

IX. Households Income and Consumption and Social Security

In 2020, the per capita disposable income nationwide was 32,189 yuan, an increase of 4.7 percent over that of the previous year or a real increase of 2.1 percent after deducting price factors. The median[47] of per capita disposable income nationwide was 27,540 yuan, up by 3.8 percent. In terms of usual residence, the per capita disposable income of urban households was 43,834 yuan, up by 3.5 percent over that of 2019, or a real growth of 1.2 percent after deducting price factors. The median of per capita disposable income of urban households was 40,378 yuan, up by 2.9 percent. The per capita disposable income of rural households was 17,131 yuan, up by 6.9 percent over that of the previous year, or 3.8 percent in real terms after deducting price factors. The median of per capita disposable income of rural households was 15,204 yuan, up by 5.7 percent. The urban-rural per capita disposable income ratio was 2.56, down by 0.08 over that of the previous year. Grouped by income quintile[48], the per capita disposable income of low-income group reached 7,869 yuan, the lower-middle-income group 16,443 yuan, the middle-income group 26,249 yuan, the upper-middle-

44. National Equities Exchange and Quotations, also called "the New Over-the-Counter Market", is a national securities exchange established upon approval by the State Council in 2012. Preferred stocks were excluded from funds raised by listed companies in National Equities Exchange and Quotations. Funds raised by shares are calculated by the disclosure date of the issurance report.

45. Corporate debenture bonds include debt financing instruments of non-financial businesses, enterprise bonds, corporate bonds and convertible bonds.

46. The premium of primary insurance received by the insurance companies refers to the premium income from primary insurance contracts confirmed by the insurance companies.

47. The median of per capita income refers to the per capita income of household lied in the middle of all surveyed households which are ranked from low to high (or high to low) based on per capita income level.

48. The income quintile refers to the five equal partitions of all surveyed households, who are ranked from low to high based on per capita income level. The top 20 percent with the highest income are classified as high-income group, and the other four levels are upper-middle-income group, middle-income group, lower-middle-income group and low-income group.

income group 41,172 yuan and the high-income group 80,294 yuan. The per capita monthly income of migrant workers was 4,072 yuan, increased by 2.8 percent over that of the previous year.

The national per capita consumption expenditure was 21,210 yuan, down by 1.6 percent over that of the previous year, or a real decrease of 4.0 percent after deducting price factors. Specifically, the per capita consumption expenditure on services[49] totaled 9,037 yuan, down by 8.6 percent over that of the previous year, accounting for 42.6 percent of the per capita consumption expenditure. In terms of usual residence, the per capita consumption expenditure of urban households was 27,007 yuan, down by 3.8 percent, or 6.0 percent in real terms after deducting price factors. The per capita consumption expenditure of rural households was 13,713 yuan, up by 2.9 percent, or a real decrease of 0.1 percent after deducting price factors. The national Engel's Coefficient stood at 30.2 percent, with that of urban and rural households standing at 29.2 percent and 32.7 percent respectively.

Figure 16: National Per Capita Disposable Income and its Growth Rates 2016-2020

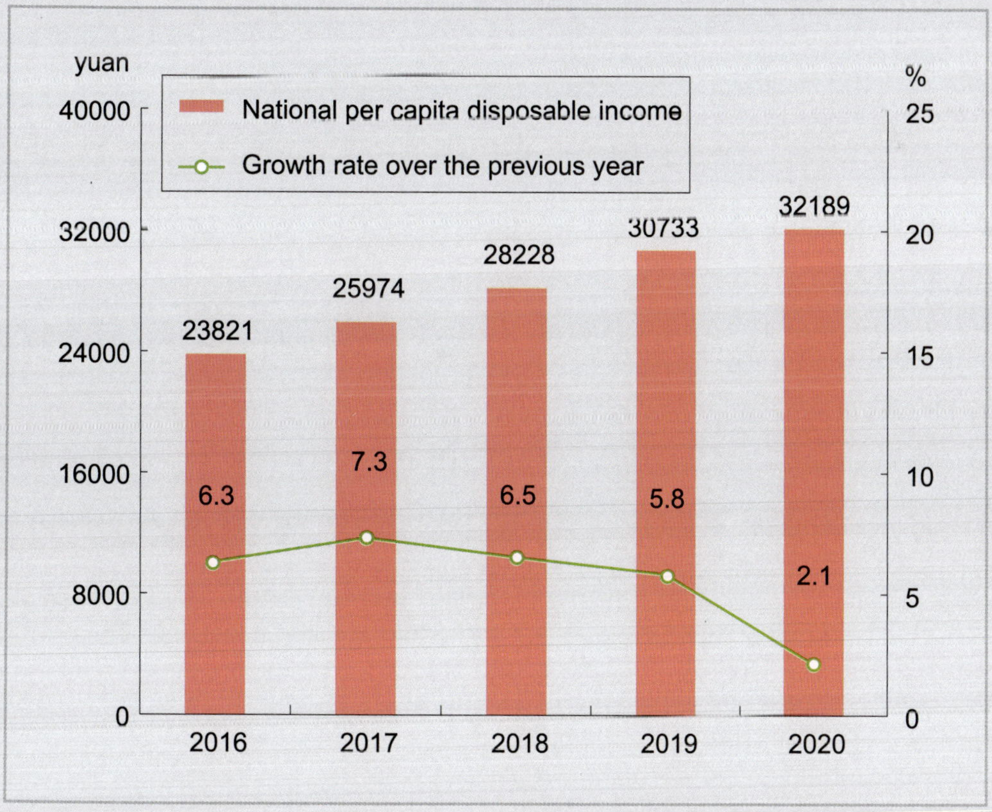

49. The consumption expenditure on services refers to the spending by households on services for daily lives including catering, education, culture and recreation and medical services.

Figure 17: National Per Capita Consumption Expenditure and Composition in 2020

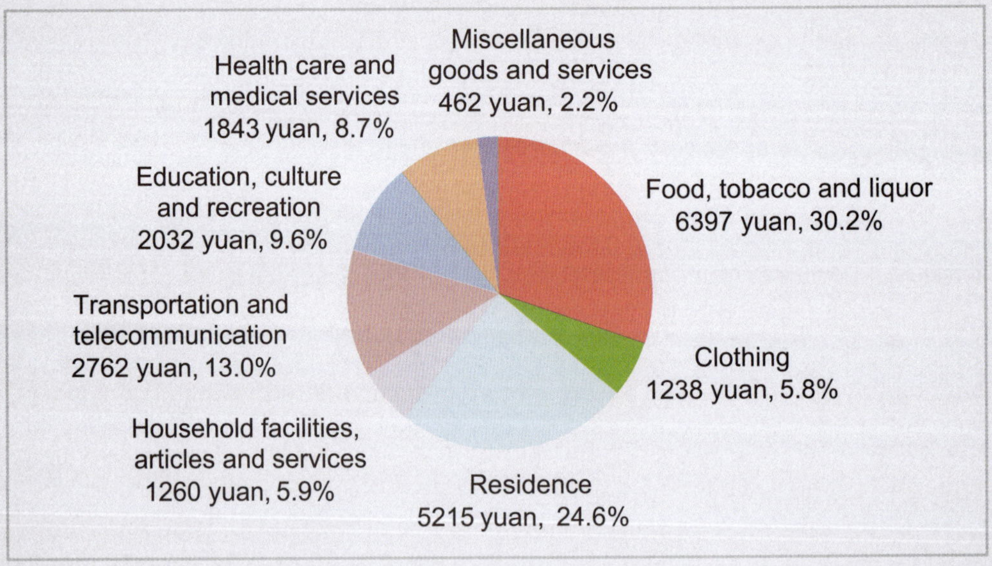

By the end of 2020, a total of 456.38 million people participated in basic endowment insurance program for urban workers, an increase of 21.50 million over that by the end of 2019. A total of 542.44 million people participated in basic endowment insurance program for urban and rural residents, an increase of 9.78 million. A total of 1,361.01 million people participated in basic medical insurance program, an increase of 6.93 million. Of this total, 344.23 million people participated in the program for workers, an increase of 14.98 million, and 1,016.78 million people participated in the program for urban and rural residents. Some 216.89 million people participated in unemployment insurance program, an increase of 11.47 million. The number of people receiving unemployment insurance payment stood at 2.70 million by the end of 2020. A total of 267.70 million people participated in work-related injury insurance, an increase of 12.91 million, of which 89.34 million were migrant workers, an increase of 3.18 million. A total of 235.46 million people participated in maternity insurance programs, an increase of 21.29 million. Minimum living allowances were granted to 8.05 million urban residents and 36.21 million rural residents, and 4.47 million rural residents living in extreme poverty[50] received relief and assistance and 13.41 million people received temporary assistance[51]. A total of 89.90 million people were financed to participate in basic medical insurance program and direct

50. Rural residents living in extreme poverty refer to the aged, the disabled and the minor under 16 years of age in rural areas who have no ability to work, no sources of income and no statutory obligors to provide for them, bring them up or support them, or whose statutory obligors have no ability to fulfill their obligations.

51. Temporary assistance refers to emergent and transitional assistance the government provides to families or individuals who experience hardships because of emergencies, unexpected harm, major diseases or other unusual factors and are not covered by other forms of social assistance programs or still suffer hardships after receiving other social assistance programs.

assistance[52] was granted to 73.00 million recipients. National subsidies and allowances were provided to 8.37 million veterans and other entitled people in 2020.

By the end of 2020, there were altogether 41 thousand social welfare institutions providing accommodation, of which 38 thousand were elderly caring organizations and 735 were children caring organizations. The social welfare institutions provided 8.509 million beds[53], of which 8.238 million were for the elderly and 98 thousand were for children. By the end of 2020, there were 29 thousand community service centers and 393 thousand community service stations.

X. Science & Technology and Education

Expenditures on research and experimental development activities (R&D) were worth 2,442.6 billion yuan in 2020, up by 10.3 percent over that of 2019, accounting for 2.40 percent of GDP. Of this total, 150.4 billion yuan was used for basic research programs. A total of 198 research projects were arranged under the national science and technology major projects and 45,700 projects were financed by the National Natural Science Foundation. By the end of 2020, there were altogether 522 state key laboratories in operation, 350 national engineering research centers (national engineering laboratories), 1,636 state-level enterprise technology centers and 212 demonstration centers for business startups and innovation. There were 1,173 state-level technology business incubators[54], and 2,386 national mass makerspaces[55]. A total of 3,639 thousand patents were authorized, up by 40.4 percent over that of the previous year. The number of PCT patent applications accepted[56] was 72 thousand. By the end of 2020, the number of patents in force was 12,193 thousand, of which 2,213 thousand were invention patents from home. The number of invention patents per 10,000 people was estimated to be 15.8. Trademark registration totaled 5,761 thousand, down by 10.1 percent over that of the previous year. A total of 550 thousand technology transfer contracts were signed, representing 2,825.2 billion yuan in value, up by 26.1 percent over that of the previous year.

52. Direct assistance includes inpatient and outpatient assistance provided by medical insurance departments and direct assistance provided by other relevant departments.

53. The beds provided by social welfare institutions include beds provided by adoption agencies, aid agencies and community agencies.

54. The state-level technology business incubators are technology-based business startup service providers consistent with the Administrative Measures for Technology Business Incubators that provide physical space, shared facilities and professional services with the mission of advancing transformation of technological achievements, cultivating technological enterprises and fostering the entrepreneurial spirit. They should be approved and accredited by the Ministry of Science and Technology.

55. The national mass makerspaces are new service platform for entrepreneurship and innovation that are in conformity with the Guidelines on Developing Mass Makerspaces and are reviewed and registered by the Ministry of Science and Technology in accordance with the Provisional Registration Regulations on National Mass Makerspaces.

56. The number of PCT patent applications accepted refers to the number of PCT patent application accepted by the State Intellectual Property Office which acts as the receiving office of PCT patent application. PCT is the abbreviation of Patent Cooperation Treaty, which is a treaty for international cooperation in the field of patents.

Figure 18: The Expenditure on Research and Experimental Development Activities (R&D) and its Growth Rates 2016-2020

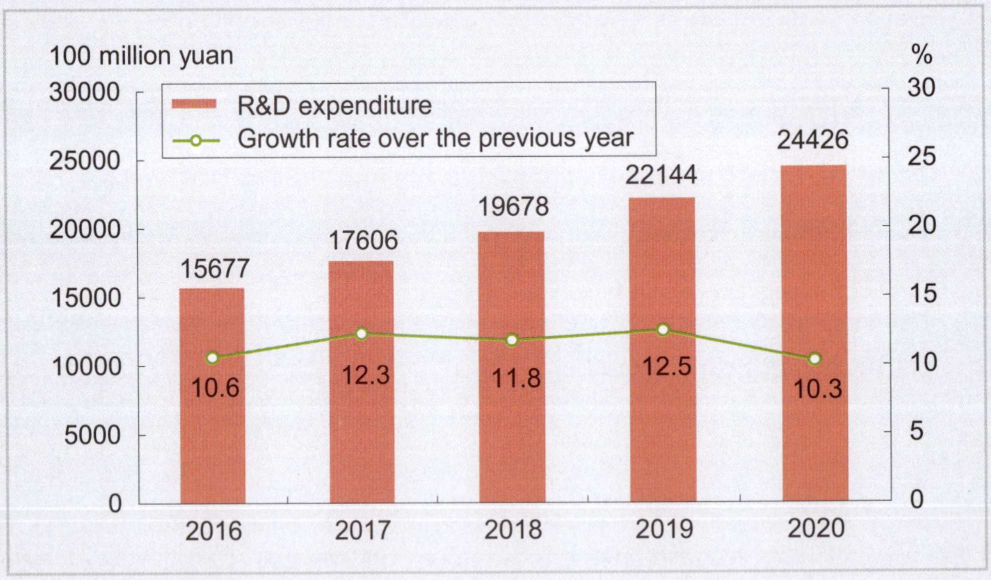

Table 15: Number of Patents Authorized and Patents in Force in 2020

Item	Patents (10,000)	Increase over 2019 (%)
Number of patents authorized	**363.9**	**40.4**
Of which: domestic	350.4	42.6
Of which: for new inventions	53.0	17.1
Of which: domestic	43.4	22.5
Number of patents in force at the end of the year	**1219.3**	**25.4**
Of which: domestic	1111.5	27.9
Of which: for new inventions	305.8	14.5
Of which: domestic	221.3	18.8

The year 2020 saw 35 times of successful satellite launches. The successful launch of Chang'e-5 brought home moon samples for the first time, and China's first Mars exploration mission named Tianwen-1 was successfully launched. The Five-hundred-meter Aperture Spherical Radio Telescope (FAST) project officially went online. China's Beidou-3 Navigation Satellite System was officially commissioned. The quantum computer prototype "Jiuzhang" was successfully created. The full-depth deep-sea manned submersible "Fendouzhe" successfully completed the 10,000-meter sea trial.

By the end of 2020, there were altogether 852 national quality inspection centers. There were 724 agencies for product quality and management system and service certification, accumulatively 790,000 enterprises were certified. A total of 2,252 national standards were developed or revised in the year, including 1,584 new standards. The qualification rate of manufactured products[57] reached 93.39 percent.

In 2020, the post-graduate education enrollment was 3,140 thousand students with 1.107 million new students and 729 thousand graduates. The general tertiary education enrollment was 32.853 million students with 9.675 million new students and 7.972 million graduates. Vocational secondary schools[58] had 16.634 million enrolled students, including 6.447 million new entrants, and 4.849 million graduates. Senior secondary schools had 24.945 million enrolled students, including 8.764 million new entrants, and 7.865 million graduates. Students enrolled in junior secondary schools totaled 49.141 million, including 16.321 million new entrants, and 15.353 million graduates. The country had a primary education enrollment of 107.254 million students, including 18.081 million new entrants, and 16.403 million graduates. There were 881 thousand students enrolled in special education schools, with 149 thousand new entrants and 121 thousand graduates. Kindergartens accommodated 48.183 million children. The number of students graduating from compulsory education reached 95.2 percent of the total enrollment, and the gross enrollment ratio for senior secondary education reached 91.2 percent.

Figure 19: Enrollment in Education 2016-2020

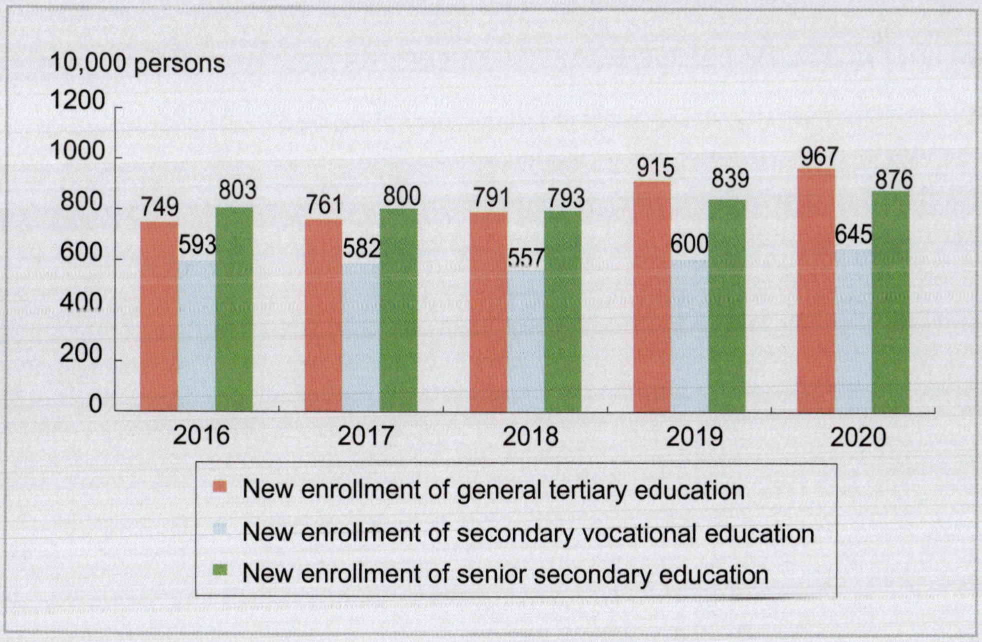

57. The qualification rate of manufactured products is the ratio of the samples that have passed the sampling quality test, the process of which follows certain methods, procedure and standard, to the total amount of the sampled products. The survey samples cover 29 sectors of the manufacturing industry.

58. Vocational secondary schools include regular specialized secondary schools, adult specialized secondary schools, vocational high schools and skilled workers schools.

XI. Culture and Tourism, Public Health and Sports

By the end of 2020, there were 2,027 art-performing groups and 3,510 museums in the culture and tourism system throughout China. A total of 3,203 public libraries received[59] 569.53 million people. There were 3,327 cultural centers. Subscribers to cable television programs numbered 210 million, in which 201 million subscribed to digital cable television programs. By the end of 2020, radio broadcasting and television broadcasting coverage rates were 99.4 percent and 99.6 percent respectively. A total of 7,476 episodes of 202 TV series and 116,688 minutes of TV cartoons were made in 2020. The country produced 531 feature movies and 119 popular science movies, documentaries, animation and special movies[60]. A total of 27.7 billion copies of newspapers and 2.0 billion copies of magazines were issued, and 10.1 billion copies of books were published. The average number of books possessed per person[61] was estimated to be 7.24 copies. By the end of the year, there were 4,234 archives in China and 176.59 million files were made accessible to the public. The business revenue of enterprises above the designated size engaged in culture and related industries reached 9,851.4 billion yuan, up by 2.2 percent over that of the previous year on a comparable basis.

The year 2020 registered 2.88 billion domestic tourists, down by 52.1 percent over that of the previous year. Of this total, there were 2.07 billion tourists from urban areas, a decrease of 53.8 percent; and 810 million tourists from rural areas, a decrease of 47.0 percent. Domestic tourism revenue was 2,228.6 billion yuan, down by 61.1 percent. Of this total, tourists from urban areas spent 1,796.7 billion yuan, down by 62.2 percent; and tourists from rural areas spent 432.0 billion yuan, down by 55.7 percent.

59. The people received by the public libraries refer to the number of people who visit libraries and use library services in the year, including borrowing and reading books, consultation and attending readers' programs.

60. Special movies refer to those using different display modes in terms of projection techniques, equipment and program as compared with the ordinary cinemas, such as IMAX movies, 3D movies, 4D movies, multidimensional movies and full dome movies.

61. The average number of books possessed per person refers to the average number of books published in the year that can be possessed per person in China.

Figure 20: The Person-times of Domestic Tourists and its Growth Rates 2016-2020

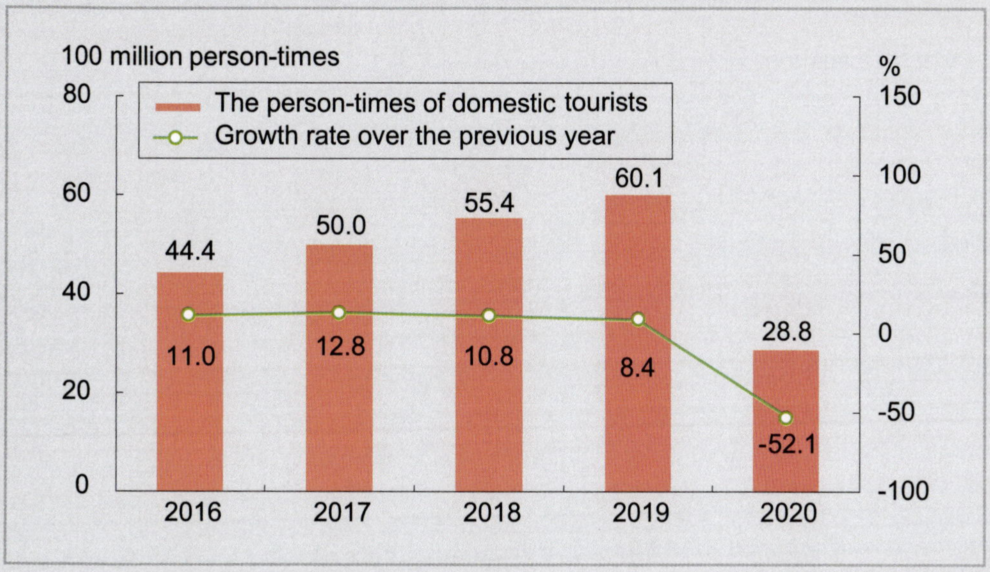

By the end of 2020, there were 1,023,000 medical and health institutions in China, including 35,000 hospitals. Of all the hospitals, 12,000 were public, and 24,000 were private. Of the 971,000 medical and health institutions at grass-root level, there were 36,000 town and township health centers, 35,000 community health service centers, 290,000 clinics and 610,000 village clinics. Of the 14,000 professional public health institutions, 3,384 were disease control and prevention centers and 2,736 were health monitoring institutions. By the end of 2020, there were 10.66 million medical technical personnel in China, including 4.08 million licensed doctors and licensed assistant doctors and 4.71 million registered nurses. The medical and health institutions in China possessed 9.11 million beds, of which, hospitals possessed 7.13 million and township health centers had 1.39 million. The total number of medical visits[62] and hospital discharges[63] in 2020 reached 7.82 billion and 230 million respectively. By the end of 2020, a total of 87,071 confirmed cases of COVID-19 had been reported nationwide, 82,067 infected had been cured and discharged from hospital, and 4,634 people died. A total of 8,177 medical and health institutions across the country provide nucleic acid testing services, with daily nucleic acid testing capacity reached 11.53 million.

62. The total number of medical visits refers to the number of people receiving medical services, including outpatient services, emergency treatment, home visits, appointment-based diagnosis and treatment, health check-up of a specific item, and health consultation and guidance (excluding health lectures).

63. The number of hospital discharges refers to the number of inpatients discharged from hospitals in the reporting period, including those who are discharged from hospitals or transferred to other medical institutions following doctors' advice, discharged from hospitals without doctors' permission, dead or other situations. The number of people who are recovered from family sickbeds is excluded.

Figure 21: Year-end Number of Medical Technical Personnel 2016-2020

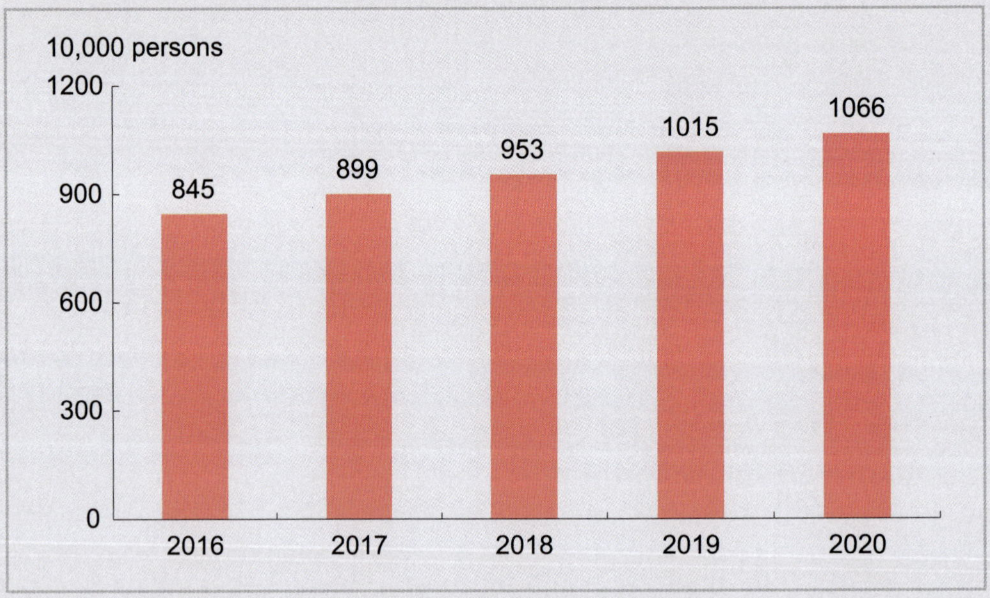

There were altogether 3.713 million sports venues[64]. The sports venue area[65] totaled 3.10 billion square meters and the per capita sports venue area was estimated to be 2.20 square meters. In 2020, Chinese athletes won 4 world championships in 3 sports events and broke 1 world record[66]. Chinese physically-challenged athletes won 24 world championships in 6 international sports competitions[67]. The year 2020 saw 37.2 percent of people aged 7 and above frequently participated in physical exercises[68].

XII. Resources, Environment and Emergency Management

In 2020, the total supply of state-owned land for construction use[69] was 658 thousand hectares, an increase of 5.5 percent over that of the previous year. Of this total, the supply for mining storage was 167 thousand hectares, up by 13.6 percent; that for real estate[70] was 155 thousand hectares, up by 9.3 percent; and that for infrastructure facilities was 337 thousand hectares, up by 0.3 percent.

64. The sports venues belonging to armed forces and railway system are excluded in the census on sports venues.

65. The sports venue area refers to area used for physical training, sports competitions and physical fitness.

66. The year 2020 has seen a significant decline of international sports events due to COVID-19, and the number of Chinese athletes winning world championships and setting world records has decreased compared with previous years.

67. Data covers the international sports events from January to March 2020 (participation in international events was suspended since April 2020 due to COVID-19).

68. The proportion of people who frequently participate in physical exercises comes from the National Fitness Activities Survey in 2020. People who frequently participate in physical exercises refer to those who participate in physical exercises at least 3 times a week, with each time lasting for at least 30 minutes and having a moderate intensity and above.

69. Total supply of state-owned land for construction use refers to the total amount of state-owned land for construction use with the land-use right transferred, allocated or leased to units or individuals through signed transaction contracts and allocation decisions by the municipal or county governments according to annual land supply plan and in line with relevant laws in the reporting period.

70. Land used for real estate refers to the sum of land used for commercial service and for residence.

The total stock of water resources in 2020 was 3,096.3 billion cubic meters.

In 2020, the total area of afforestation reached 6.77 million hectares, of which 2.89 million hectares were afforested by manpower, accounting for 42.7 percent of the total. The land area improved by grass plantation[71] was 2.83 million hectares. By the end of 2020, there were 474 national natural reserves. A total of 60 thousand square kilometers of land have been saved from soil erosion.

Preliminary estimation indicated that the total energy consumption in 2020 amounted to 4.98 billion tons of standard coal equivalent, up by 2.2 percent over that of 2019. The consumption of coal increased by 0.6 percent; crude oil, up by 3.3 percent; natural gas, up by 7.2 percent; and electric power, up by 3.1 percent. The consumption of coal accounted for 56.8 percent of the total energy consumption, 0.9 percentage point lower than that of 2019, while clean energy consumption, such as natural gas, hydropower, nuclear power and wind power accounted for 24.3 percent, 1.0 percentage point higher. The comprehensive energy consumption per unit calcium carbide by key energy-intensive industrial enterprises went down by 2.1 percent, per unit synthetic ammonia up by 0.3 percent, per ton steel down by 0.3 percent and per unit electrolytic aluminium down by 1.0 percent. The standard coal consumption per kilowatt-hour of thermal power generation decreased by 0.6 percent. The carbon dioxide emission per 10,000 yuan worth of GDP was cut by 1.0 percent.

Figure 22: The Proportion of Clean Energy Consumption in the Total Energy Consumption 2016-2020

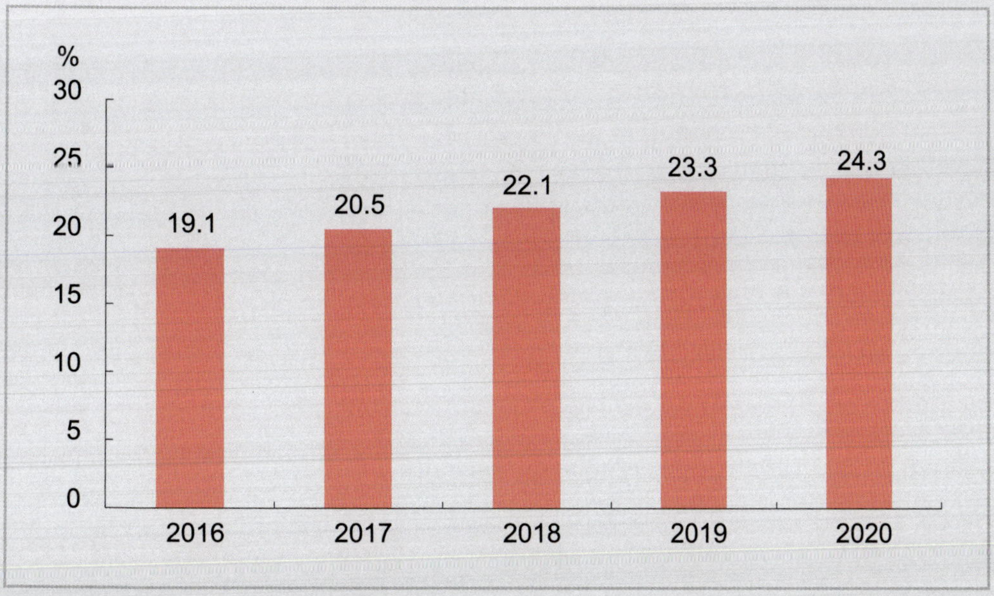

71. The land area improved by grass plantation refers to the area of increased forage grass by adopting measures such as sowing and cultivation plus the area where primitive vegetation and the ecology of grasslands have been improved by measures such as restraining the content of salt, alkali and sand, improving the quality of soil and fencing the forests.

Area of offshore oceanic water[72] met the national quality standard Grade I and II accounted for 77.4 percent; that met Grade III standard 7.7 percent; and water of Grade IV or inferior quality 14.9 percent.

Of the 324 cities subject to noise monitoring program, 4.3 percent enjoyed fairly good environment, 66.4 percent had good environment, 28.7 percent had fair environment, 0.6 percent had poor environment in downtown areas.

The average temperature in 2020 was 10.25℃, down by 0.09℃ compared with that of the previous year. Typhoons hit China 5 times in 2020.

In 2020, natural disasters hit 19.96 million hectares of crops, of which 2.71 million hectares of crops were demolished. Flood, waterlogging and geological disasters caused a direct economic loss of 268.6 billion yuan. Droughts caused a direct economic loss of 24.9 billion yuan. Disasters caused by low temperature, frost and snow made a total direct economic loss of 15.4 billion yuan. Oceanic disasters caused a direct economic loss of 800 million yuan. The country recorded 20 earthquakes with magnitude 5.0 and over, 5 of which caused disasters, causing a direct economic loss about 1.8 billion yuan. The year 2020 witnessed 1,153 forest fires, with 9 thousand hectares of forests damaged.

The death toll due to work accidents amounted to 27,412 people. Work accidents in industrial, mining and commercial companies caused 1.301 deaths out of every 100 thousand employees, down by 11.7 percent over that of 2019. The death toll for one million tons of coal produced in coalmines was 0.059 people, down by 28.9 percent. The road traffic death toll per 10 thousand vehicles was 1.66 people, down by 7.8 percent.

Data Sources:

In this Communiqué, data of newly increased employed people in urban areas, registered unemployment rate in urban areas, social security and skilled workers schools are from the Ministry of Human Resources and Social Security; data of foreign exchange reserves and exchange rates are from the State Administration of Foreign Exchange; data of environment monitoring and the carbon dioxide emission per 10,000 yuan worth of GDP are from the Ministry of Ecology and Environment; data of finance are from the Ministry of

72. Offshore oceanic water quality is evaluated by the area method.

Finance; data of market entities, quality inspection, the formulation and revision of national standards and qualification rate of manufactured products are from the State Administration for Market Regulation; data of output of aquatic products and area of farmland newly equipped with effective water-saving irrigation systems are from the Ministry of Agriculture and Rural Affairs; data of production of timber, area of afforestation, land area improved by grass plantation, and national natural reserves are from the National Forestry and Grassland Administration; data of area of farmland newly equipped with irrigation system, water resources and land newly saved from soil erosion are from the Ministry of Water Resources; data of installed power generation capacity, new power transformer equipment with a capacity of 220 kilovolts and above and electricity consumption are from the China Electricity Council; data of volume of freight handled by ports, container shipping of ports, highway transportation, waterway transportation, new and rebuilt highways and new throughput capacity of berths for over 10,000-tonnage ships are from the Ministry of Transport; data of railway transportation, new railways put into operation, new double-track railways put into operation and electrified railways put into operation are from China Railway; data of civil aviation and new civil transportation airports are from the Civil Aviation Administration of China; data of motor vehicles for civilian use and traffic accidents are from the Ministry of Public Security; data of postal service are from the State Post Bureau; data of telecommunication, software revenue, and new lines of optical-fiber cables are from the Ministry of Industry and Information Technology; data of internet users and internet coverage are from China Internet Network information Center; data of housing units rebuilt or renovated in rundown urban areas and for poverty-stricken rural households with economic status registered at the local governments in the fight against poverty are from the Ministry of Housing and Urban-Rural Development; data of imports and exports of goods are from the General Administration of Customs; data of imports and exports of services, foreign direct investment, outbound direct investment, overseas contracted projects and overseas labor contracts are from the Ministry of Commerce; data of tax and fee cuts are from the State Taxation Administration; data of monetary finance and corporate debenture bonds are from the People's Bank of China; data of funds raised through domestic exchange markets are from China Securities Regulatory Commission; data of the insurance sector are from China Banking and Insurance Regulatory Commission; data of medical insurance, maternity insurance, people financed to participate in basic medical insurance program, and direct assistance recipients are from the National Healthcare and Security Administration; data of urban and rural minimum living allowances, relief and assistance granted to rural residents living in extreme poverty, temporary assistance and social services are from the Ministry of Civil Affairs; data of entitled people are from the Ministry of

Veterans Affairs; data of national science and technology major projects, state key laboratories, state-level technology business incubators, national mass makerspaces and technology transfer contracts are from the Ministry of Science and Technology; data of natural science foundation projects are from the National Natural Science Foundation; data of national engineering research centers (national engineering laboratories), enterprise technical centers and demonstration centers for business startups and innovation are from the National Development and Reform Commission; data of patents and trademarks are from the National Intellectual Property Administration; data of satellite launches are from the State Administration of Science, Technology and Industry for National Defense; data of education are from the Ministry of Education; data of art-performing groups, museums, public libraries, cultural centers and tourism are from the Ministry of Culture and Tourism; data of television and radio programs are from the National Radio and Television Administration; data of movies are from the China Film Administration; data of newspapers, magazines and books are from the National Press and Publication Administration; data of files are from the State Archives Administration; data of medical care and health are from the National Health Commission; data of sports are from the General Administration of Sport; data of physically-challenged athletes are from the China Disabled Persons' Federation; data of supply of state-owned land for construction use and direct economic loss caused by oceanic disasters are from the Ministry of Natural Resources; data of average temperature and typhoons are from the China Meteorological Administration; data of areas of crops hit by natural disasters, direct economic loss caused by flood, waterlogging and geological disasters, direct economic loss caused by droughts, direct economic loss caused by low temperature, frost and snow, forest fires, areas of forests damaged and workplace accidents are from the Ministry of Emergency Management; data of the number of earthquakes and direct economic loss caused by earthquakes are from the China Earthquake Administration; all the other data are from the National Bureau of Statistics.

In case of any differences between English translation and the original Chinese text, the Chinese edition shall prevail.